"*Reconstructing Dad* is the fruit of years of thoughtful reflection, and Chuck Ammons is the perfect pastor to write such a work. A gifted teacher and one of the most articulate communicators I know, Chuck brings clarity to the seeming contradictions in Scripture with grace and insight. As you journey through this book, you will find your heart stirred and your love for God the Father deepened, because you'll see Him so beautifully reflected in the Son. This isn't just a book of theological insight—it's a transformative work born from both the Word and Chuck's own life. He writes not merely to expose truth, but to invite readers into it. His authenticity as a father and pastor shines through every page. You'll be inspired to grow in your understanding, trust, and love for your heavenly Father in powerful new ways. Dive in—you will not be disappointed."

— **DAVID OATES**, Executive Director, Church United Tampa Bay
Lead Pastor, SeaGlass Church

"*Reconstructing Dad* is a gift of clarity to followers of Jesus. One of the primary reasons Jesus came was to paint humanity a clearer picture of who God actually is. He's our Father in heaven. For many of us, the personification of a Father elicits feelings of warmth and joy. Unfortunately, over a quarter of American kids grow up without a dad in their home. It's easy to see how this analogy can be problematic...Drawing from his own experiences, both of having a dad and being a dad, [Chuck] reconstructs our misconceptions about our Father in heaven, and gives a way to experience His love in a new, profound way!"

— **DR. JASON BURNS**, Lead Pastor, Access Church

"This book feels like a warm conversation with someone who's been where you are. Chuck gently deconstructs our warped views of God and helps us rebuild our faith on the rock-solid truth that the Father has always looked like Jesus."

— **CAESAR KALINOWSKI**, church planter, missional strategist
and author of *Transformed: A New Way of Being Christian*

"If you're new to Chuck's teaching and style, I'm thrilled for you. Thrilled like when a young person hears a classic rock guitar riff for the first time. Chuck has consistently and skillfully unraveled the gospel from the complications of religion and presented it in such an accessible manner that living it is actually not only possible, but a welcomed joy. This book addresses some of the most pervasive roadblocks to intimacy with God, such as, "Did a mean God suddenly get nice when Jesus showed up?" Issues people have with the Old Testament revelation of God are dealt with beautifully and profoundly. You will see your Father exactly as Jesus put Him on display. Thanks for writing this book, Chuck! This is going to disciple many into wholeness."

— **BILL VANDERBUSH**, author of
Unveiled Horizon: Reflections on the Nature of God

"I cannot think of anything more important or foundational in life than understanding—or better yet, encountering—God as Father. Chuck is a true shepherd with God's heart for you and a profound depth in the Scriptures. Knowing God as our Father, and all that implies, could end wars, heal relationships, and bring security and joy even to the most troubled souls. It will launch you into your calling as you come to terms with these unimaginably wonderful truths. I encourage you to read this book and embark on the most profound journey into the nature of God. It will be life-changing!"

— **DAVID BRADSHAW**, President & Founder, Awaken the Dawn
Executive Director, Communion America

"In *Reconstructing Dad*, Chuck uses the artistry of language to bring the true being of God out of the fog of our worn-out experience and into the clarity of His divine essence. I love how Chuck confronts our wrong views of Abba. He exposes the underbelly of our core issues with the hand of a linguistic physician and he breaks down the gates of fear and torment with statements like, "God does not populate heaven by the fear of hell, but by the beauty of Christ." I highly recommend you take a serious dive into this work...Chuck is one of the most Christlike people I know, and I could not urge you more strongly to absorb what he has to say in *Reconstructing Dad*."

— **CALEB HYERS**, Senior Leader, The Resting Place
and author of *Common Unity* and *Living in Dependenceville*

"A wonderful piece of writing and theology, covering vast biblical distance, and reflecting on one of the most important relationships shaping both our inner and outer world. Chuck has given us a gift that promises a renewed vision of God and His heart for us."

— **BRIAN SANDERS**, founder, Underground Network
and author of *The 6 Seasons of Calling*

"If you've ever struggled with doubts or wondered whether God is truly good and near, *Reconstructing Dad* is a beautiful invitation to see God as He really is. With theological depth and pastoral warmth, my friend Chuck Ammons paints a compelling picture of a Father who doesn't look like our wounds—but looks exactly like Jesus. Through Scripture, Chuck helps readers confront distorted views of God, dismantle orphan-hearted faith, and rediscover the Father's heart of love, mercy, and justice. Chuck has been making an incredible difference in our community for years, inspiring people to live life to the overflow—and this book is a powerful extension of that ministry. I'm so thankful for his leadership and voice on this timely and important topic."

— **DR. DANIEL BUTSON**, Lead Pastor, Fellowship Church

"When you pray, who do you pray to? God? Jesus? Holy Spirit? Lord? Father? If that last one struck a nerve, you picked up the right book. *Reconstructing Dad* is a breathtakingly restorative journey into the heart of a good, good Father God who has always been closer, kinder, and more merciful than we dared imagine. With raw vulnerability and profound insight, my spiritual "big brother" Chuck Ammons dismantles the orphan spirit, offering a fresh lens to see the Father's unchanging love through the life and work of Jesus. If you've ever wrestled with questions about God's character or struggled to reconcile your earthly father wounds with His perfect love, this book will meet you where you are and lead you toward healing. Bold, compassionate, and deeply transformative, this is a must-read for anyone longing to know their Father's heart."

— **BRIT EATON**, co-author of *Reckless Grace*
and *The Uncovery: Understanding the Power of Community to Heal Trauma*

"*Reconstructing Dad* is not just a theological correction—it's a pastoral invitation to healing. Chuck addresses the deep confusion many carry about the character of God and carefully reconstructs our understanding through the person of Jesus. This book is both theologically sound and deeply personal, offering a way forward for anyone disillusioned by distorted images of God."

— **GEORGE A. WOOD**, author of
The Uncovery: Understanding the Power of Community to Heal Trauma

"Are you wanting to experience God as a good, good Father? Find a comfy chair and a good cup of coffee, and begin your journey reading *Reconstructing Dad*. You will find in this book what you've always been looking for...a heavenly Father who sees you, pursues you, and adores you. Chuck Ammons is able to go both deep and practical with personal stories and insightful illustrations. You will enjoy this book, as it transforms your understanding of God as Father."

— **LEN HARPER**, Senior Pastor, Overflow Church
Leader, Minister's Connection

"*Reconstructing Dad* is not just a book—it is an invitation into healing. As I read these pages, I found myself both challenged and comforted, confronted and restored. Chuck Ammons has written a work that is both theologically rich and deeply practical. For anyone who has grown up without a healthy picture of fatherhood, this book does not offer shallow answers—it offers a faithful path home. What moved me most is how clearly the Father's heart is revealed through the lens of Jesus. This book carries a timely prophetic relevance for a generation wrestling with fatherlessness, identity, and belonging. It is a specific word for a specific moment, and I believe it will bring healing to many who did not even know they were still wounded. *Reconstructing Dad* helped me personally, and I am confident it will help countless others encounter the love of Father God in a way that transforms both their theology and their hearts."

— **DR. BRENT SIMPSON**, Lead Pastor, Arise Church
and Founder of the Arise Network

"As a professional counselor, pastor, and dad, I have to say that this book is gold. As a counselor, I know that the brokenness of our past so often reaches into our present, disrupting the relationships we deeply desire. Chuck does a wonderful job of exposing the potential we all have to let our past impact our present—without the admonition coming across as a therapy session. As a pastor, Chuck does a masterful job of leading the reader through what this world communicates in unhealthy ways that so often shape the word *dad*. Chuck then leads the reader to our heavenly Father to redefine God's original intent—and to me, this is as sweet as it gets. And as a dad, I have a deep desire to continue meeting the needs of my children and grandchildren, and this longing permeates the content in a way that draws the reader in. Being a son to the Father in heaven is the most equipping pursuit a dad can have, and this is explained so very well. *Reconstructing Dad* is a valuable read for men and women alike—for all who want to understand the heart of the Father."

— **DAVID SPEICHER**, Senior Pastor, South Bay Church
Author, *Not Many Days From Now*

"Both in and out of the church, our world today can't seem to make its mind up about who God is. An angry, vengeful voice in the sky or a counter-cultural hippie in the desert? But what if God is something altogether different? More powerful, more gracious, more mysterious and intentional than we could imagine. In *Reconstructing Dad*, Chuck invites us to both seek and find this heart of the Father on every page of the Bible. (It's also nice to find a theological book written in language I can actually understand!)"

— **ANDREW OSENGA**, Songwriter, Musician, Record Producer
Author, *How To Remember*

Chuck Ammons's writing reliably conveys solid-gold Truth, yet at the same time, he writes with a pizzazz and lively energy that touches our heart, our soul and our daily life. This latest masterpiece offers in each chapter a laser focus on the biblical reality of God's fatherly love and purpose. Taken to heart, this flow of Truth will transform us forever. One word sums up the impact: Wow!

— **DR. THOMAS E. WOODWARD**, Founder, Apologetics, Inc.
Fellow, The Discovery Institute, Author, *Doubts About Darwin*

Chuck Ammons has put together a heartfelt and much-needed book that addresses the deeply important subject of what the Father Heart of God looks like. He skillfully confronts the distortions that so many people carry concerning their view of God. As a missionary who works with and trains disciples and pastors from across Africa, I often encounter people with distorted views of God and His ways. I myself struggled with this for many years. Many believers love Jesus but live with an underlying fear that the Father is angry, unapproachable, and ready to smite them at any moment of wrongdoing. *Reconstructing Dad*, written with pastoral care and biblical truth, dismantles these false perceptions and rebuilds a true image of God, rooted in grace, mercy, compassion, and love. Every chapter feels like a breath of fresh air. This is a timely and necessary book for the church today. If you desire to know God more deeply and for who He really is, and if you are ready to trade in fear and anxiousness for sonship and joy, then this book is for you. God willing, copies will be traveling with me around the world to hand out to students and pastors.

— ANDRÉ DE VRIES, Founder and Director of
Africa 4 Jesus – School of Discipleship

Growing up with a single mom, I immediately gravitated to God as father. I even began writing a book about it. I'm glad I didn't finish it. Chuck Ammons has written a far better book on the topic than I would have. With wit, wisdom, and whimsy, he diagnoses our many father wounds, tears down lies and misunderstandings about God, and brings us on a journey to meet the joyful and loving God of Scripture—the Father who delights in us, who seeks to bless us, who longs to father us. But this book is much more than that, too. Chuck equips readers with the skills necessary to find their heavenly Father in the face of common distortions about God. This is a book that will not only enlighten you, but one I believe you will return to again and again. I wish he had written it thirty years ago."

— DAN KENT, author, *Confident Humility:
Becoming Your Full Self Without Becoming Full of Yourself*

ReCONSTRUCTING DAD

SEEING GOD THROUGH THE LENS OF JESUS

CHUCK AMMONS

CR Cross River
COLBY, KANSAS USA

RECONSTRUCTING DAD

Paperback ISBN: 978-1-936501-95-3

Hardcover ISBN: 978-1-936501-96-0

 Published by CrossRiver Media Group, Colby, Kansas. CrossRiverMedia.com

For more on Chuck Ammons, please visit ChuckAmmons.com.

Editors: Debra L. Butterfield, Andy Lee, and Robin Melvin

Cover and Interior Designer: Tamara Clymer

Cover Photography: Photo ID 135896218 © Yufa12379 | Dreamstime.com

Printed in the United States of America.

To my earthly dad...
You named me before I was born and you always wanted me.
Though you were gone too soon, I can't wait to dance with you
one day before Jesus! Your legacy is alive and strong.

To my step-dad...
Thank you for cheering me on and teaching me redneck golf.

To my spiritual dad, Len, and my big brother, Chris...
I love and lead like I do because you've loved
and led me so completely. I am eternally grateful!

To my heavenly Dad...
When You opened my eyes to see Your adoration
and how You've always pursued me as my Father,
You wrecked my world in the most beautiful way.
My every breath, my every thought, my every desire is You.
Thank You for this adventure we get to share.
It just keeps on getting better!

CONTENTS

Foreword 13

Introduction: Life as a House 15

1. Fatherless 21

2. My Two (Schizophrenic) Dads 33

3. Dad Looks Just Like Jesus 43

4. Hold What You've Got 57

5. Conflicting Kingdoms 65

6. Foggy Pots and Funhouse Mirrors 75

7. This is My Son. Listen to Him. 101

8. Missing the Mark and Missing the Point 113

9. God is Not the Godfather 133

10. Terminator Jesus? 149

11. Just Right 163

12. Justice as Restorative Love 181

Conclusion 195

A Prayer to My Father 205

Acknowledgments....................207

About the Author....................209

Endnotes....................213

FOREWORD

THERE ARE MOMENTS when a book feels less like a read and more like a homecoming. *Reconstructing Dad* is that kind of book.

In these pages, Pastor Chuck Ammons extends more than words—he extends a hand. A hand that reaches into the ache of spiritual disillusionment, into the questions that polite religion often silences, and into the deep longing so many of us carry as we ask these questions:

Is God truly good?

Is He really like Jesus?

And if so, can I trust Him with my whole heart?

With the honesty of someone who's wrestled in the dark and the wisdom of one who's found light worth sharing, Chuck invites us on a renovation journey—not of religion, but of relationship. He walks us through the house of our faith, room by room, not to tear it down in anger, but to lovingly restore it with truth. Not abstract doctrine, but truth incarnate: Jesus, the visible image of the invisible God.

What makes this book so compelling is not only its theological clarity, but its compassionate tone. First, it's written by a wonderful dad. Chuck loves his family, I mean, really loves his family! And he loves the family of God. He's written this amazing book for those whose view of the Father has been shaped by absence, performance, fear, or disappointment. It's written for those who are ready to dismantle damaging narratives, not to destroy faith, but to rebuild it on something solid, on Someone sure.

Chuck's own story, his experiences as a dad and a pastor, and his deep reverence for Scripture all converge in this work, offering a kind of spiritual therapy for the soul. He doesn't shy away from the hard questions, but he also never leaves us there. He brings us back, again and again, to the Jesus who said, "If you've seen Me, you've seen the Father."

So, if you've ever felt the subtle ache of spiritual orphanhood or carried quiet questions beneath the surface of your belief, this book is a gentle invitation to return, reimagine, and rediscover the Father who has always looked like Jesus—and who has always been closer than you dared to hope.

Welcome home.

Dr. Brian Simmons
Lead Translator, *The Passion Translation*
Passion & Fire Ministries

INTRODUCTION

LIFE AS A HOUSE

I STOOD INSIDE THE OPEN DOORWAY of our home horrified. The needs of our growing family of seven had forced a decision. Move or remodel. So, with the help of a contractor friend, we drew up a dream renovation and dove in. Now the very spot where my wife and I pictured raising our kids looked unrecognizable.

Walls were moved, the kitchen was gutted, and an entire wing of the house was off-limits to prepare for a new master suite. We had hired a nationally recognized flooring company expecting quick, quality work. My wife and kids moved to my mom's home until the house was livable again, as I stayed to oversee the project. That had been weeks ago, and our dream was quickly turning into a nightmare.

The flooring crew arrived late on their first day and then left early. They chipped up old tiles, leaving piles scattered across rooms like life-sized ant colonies. They continued this unorthodox routine until I arrived home from a long day of work to find they'd laid one-third of our flooring…except. They had laid every tile unevenly. Every. Single. One. The wood grain planks, meant to create a seamless appearance, looked like a drunken staircase of jagged edges. I stood in disbelief.

For a moment, I considered hiding the floor with area rugs. But this was our foundation. If it were ever to be a home worthy for my kids to grow up in, we needed to tear it up and start over.

When it comes to our relationship with God, building upon the right foundation is everything. The apostle Paul wrote, "By the grace

God has given me, I laid a foundation as a wise builder, and someone else is building on it. But each one should build with care" (1 Corinthians 3:10 NIV). Your view of God as Father is the foundation on which you are building your life. And that foundation was largely shaped by the physical and spiritual house you grew up in.

YOUR VIEW OF GOD IS SHAPED BY THE PHYSICAL HOUSE YOU GREW UP IN.

God refers to Himself as our Father and declares He longs for us like a momma bird protects her babies under her wing (Matthew 23:37). He designed family to be a safe, tangible expression of His love and protection. That was the plan.

But sin invaded the story, distorting our lens with an incomplete picture of His heart at best and an immoral one at worst. Many have suffered under the neglect or abuse of parents who bore His name but failed to reflect His heart. That distortion shapes everything…how we see ourselves, what we pursue, and most significantly, how we see God as Father.

YOUR VIEW OF GOD IS SHAPED BY THE SPIRITUAL HOUSE YOU GREW UP IN

I have heard many people say, "The Bible says it. I believe it. That settles it." But the Bible was used to both defend and abolish slavery. It has stood at the center of movements for women's rights and to advocate for women to be silent in churches. People use it both to affirm and deny spiritual gifts. Beyond this, we often find contrasting images of God in its pages—a God who seems wrathful in one moment and tender in the next.

The truth is, we all read Scripture through a lens. We don't see things as they are…we see things as we are. You may emphasize certain verses and skim others based on the spiritual narrative you inherited. Just as with our physical upbringing, the spiritual image of God we received early on may be incomplete or even damaging to our hearts.

This isn't a rant against the church. As a pastor of more than twenty-five years, I love the church. This is instead an invitation to maturity. We should honor every spiritual home that helped reveal God's love to our hearts, but we will only find wholeness when we let Him draw near and reveal any beliefs we've taken on that are unworthy of the gospel.

In the pages ahead, we'll explore how God revealed Himself progressively through the Old Testament, always from behind a veil, until Jesus arrived to show us the fullness of the Father. Jesus is the Father without a veil.

He is the interpretive key to everything. We'll never understand the Old Testament, God the Father, or our own story until we see it through the lens of Jesus.

There are things you believe about God that are beautiful and true. They shine through how you live and love. But there are also places where your image of God needs renovation to bring healing and make space for where He wants to lead you.

This may challenge long-held beliefs or unspoken fears, like saying, "God is good," while living like an orphan. Or wrestling with questions about God's love and the Bible.

If God really loves me, why does He seem so silent?

How can I trust God when He allowed (fill-in-the-blank) to happen?

What about hell, wrath, and violence in the Bible?

Maybe you've pushed the pain of your questions away or tried to drown it with distraction. Such busyness is nothing more than area rugs trying to conceal a faulty foundation. Meanwhile, God invites all of us to trade our fractured images of Him for a clearer vision that transforms and fills us with hope. That's what this book is about. Before we begin, let me give you three words of encouragement for the journey.

RECONSTRUCTION REQUIRES DECONSTRUCTION

Understand, we aren't reconstructing God. He is perfect and He never changes. Instead, we're invited to renovate the lens through which we have come to see Him. The topic of deconstruction has stirred fear and confusion in many, and some of this is understandable. Crowds have used the banner of deconstruction to trade tenets of a historic faith, only to champion modern fads and the idolatry of their own opinions. They tear down theological houses but find themselves in sinking sand.

However, another far more foundational sense of deconstruction is inevitable if we are to mature in our faith. The truth is, you and I don't yet see God fully as He is. "For now we see in a mirror dimly, but then face to face. Now I know in part; then I shall know fully, even as I have been fully known" (1 Corinthians 13:12).

We each carry within us some beautiful hallways of truth that fill us with joy. And we have some closets of fear and unbelief that steal our peace. Why? Because salvation is instantaneous, but discipleship is the continual renovation of our souls, catching up with the reality that already took place in our spirits.

If you know Jesus, He's already fully redeemed you, and you are now on a journey of learning and unlearning with Him by your side. Honest evaluation of our inherited theology is essential to our spiritual growth. Jesus welcomes our questions, reminding us we aren't called to have faith in our faith, but faith in the Faithful One.

Many of us were taught that asking questions was dangerous. But trust isn't formed without questions, and you cannot place a new revelation of God on a faulty foundation. In the pages ahead, I am going to ask questions that might make you uncomfortable. I may pose questions you wish I'd left under the rug. I beg you, don't run from the discomfort. Instead, invite the Holy Spirit, your Comforter, to walk with you. And wherever He reveals uneven tiles, let Him lay new floor on your foundation.

PROGRESS OFTEN LOOKS LIKE CHAOS

As you begin to ask honest questions, it may feel like the floor is falling out from under you at times. It's okay. It feels scary because it matters to you so deeply. But it also might be a sign that you've been trying to hold things together on your own for too long. As you invite God to reveal who He truly is, with courageous honesty and without fear, He will show you He's been here all along and that your whole world is being held steady by His hands (Colossians 1:17). He's holding *you*. Don't rush putting your house back together again. Just stay honest before Him in the sawdust. Jesus is your destination. You've already arrived and He's already pleased.

YOUR FATHER LONGS FOR YOU TO FIND HIM

"You will seek me and find me, when you seek me with all your heart. I will be found by you, declares the Lord" (Jeremiah 29:13–14a).

You didn't stumble here by accident. God has been drawing you to this moment. Let Him speak for Himself and resist the urge to shape His story around what you wish He'd said…or hadn't said. Jesus is the Father's answer, and He is good!

I've been seeking, praying, and wrestling against chaos for eight years writing this book. During that time, many of the truths I've come to embrace have formed gradually in a refiner's fire. This is our Father's heart. He longs to be found by us, so we can run together in new fields of grace.

Jesus Christ is the fullness of who the Father has always been. Your decision to allow God to build this truth to maturity will be like my home renovation. It'll take time. It will be messy. Your commitment to ask honest questions, to refuse labels, and to continually choose a life of radical non-enemy-making love will cost you. It may cost your reputation or social standing in some groups. This has been true for me. But Jesus already footed the bill, and He promises to usher you into a more beautiful space with Him than you have the capacity to ask or imagine. It's worth it.

I may not know you, but my Father created you and He adores you. That makes you my brother, my sister, and my friend. Friend, I bless you! I pray our Father will move the very foundation of your being to a spacious residence alongside the Father called Mercy. The Father called Love. The Father who looks just like Jesus. May He heal old wounds, remove old carpet on the floors you've walked on for so long, and replace the tired artwork on your heart's walls.

Chuck Ammons
February 2026

ONE

FATHERLESS

The human problem is the orphan spirit

THIS CAN'T BE HAPPENING. *I was over it a long time ago. Everyone deals with loss. We all have been dealt tough cards in the hand of life. Yes. My dad died. But that was over thirty years ago. I'm okay now. Actually, I'm better than okay. I'm happy. Goodness gracious, I am a dad. I've dealt with this wound already...right?*

That's what I told myself. But the tears forming, threatening to appear at any moment, told a different story.

It had been a normal day until then. I'd gone to work as usual, come home as usual, and sat in a familiar chair in the gymnasium where my thirteen-year-old son practiced karate...as usual. This was supposed to be a quiet retreat, a safe space to read and reflect. I was preparing to lead a group of college-aged guys at our church through *Wild at Heart* by John Eldredge. Years ago, the book had changed my life, and on this evening, I found myself working through the journal that accompanied the book, the *Field Manual.*

I guess it was lost on me that a field manual was given to people headed off to war, because I sat in my chair, emotionally unarmed, grinning like an idiot. Little did I know I was walking my heart onto a literary minefield of sorrows I thought I'd escaped long ago. I read, and reread, the simplest of questions for which I had no answer.

"What was your father like emotionally?"

"What did he like to do?"

"Was he full of fun, or serious?"

"Was he a man of great adventure, willing to take risks?"[1]

Like the end of a movie with an unexpected plot twist, I sat dumbfounded. I had to admit to myself for the first time I didn't know even the most basic information about the man whose mannerisms and features I had inherited. The father who dreamed of the day he would welcome a son into the world, and who eagerly picked out my name long before I was born. The man who set up living room forts, took my sister and me to Busch Gardens, and let us eat Easy Cheese straight out of the can.

Sure, I had acquired facts about him. I heard stories. But the first moving picture memories I can access in the vault of my mind are from just after my picture-perfect world fell apart. My first memory is from the day my mom picked my sister and me up from school to tell us, through tears, my dad had been in an accident…and he was gone. The second memory is from his funeral where I comforted grieving guests with tissues, telling them everything was going to be okay. Before that moment, all I have are faded snapshots.

I snapped back to the present when I caught a glimpse of my son gliding across the gym floor smiling at me with warm and knowing admiration. At that moment, I was forced to face the enormous weight I'd shielded myself from. I was a son who didn't know his father. And this fact shaped how I approached God as Father.

PHYSICAL FATHERLESSNESS

As I write, nearly twenty million children in the US, more than one in four, live without a biological, step, or adoptive father in the home. This number has nearly tripled since 1960. Psychologists have invested billions of dollars and hours in counseling and research, resulting in mountains of statistics pointing to the same simple truth—the absence of a father figure affects society at the most foundational level. Respected political science scholar Stephen Baskerville confirms the seriousness of this reality. He wrote, "Virtually every major social pathology has been linked to fatherless children: violent crime, drug and alcohol abuse, truancy, unwed pregnancy, suicide, and psychological disorders—all correlating more strongly with fatherlessness than with any other single factor, (surpassing even race and poverty)."[2]

Statistically, those without dads are far more likely to face poverty, substance abuse, behavioral disorders, and incarceration. But this isn't about statistics. It's about stories. I don't share this to shame anyone but simply to state the obvious. Dads matter.

Our own experience with our earthly fathers, for better or worse, shapes our view of God as Father. And to my fellow dads, I ask you to consider that your current approach to parenting is unavoidably linked to how you think God is fathering you. Every action of patience or anger, intimacy or distance, grace or threat reflects who you think your Father-God is and how you think He relates to you.

Our expectations of our kids bear a striking resemblance to what we think God expects of us. The way we speak and respond reveals what is happening in our hearts (Luke 6:45). This matters because children who feel unseen or unsafe with their fathers often carry an orphan mentality into their relationship with God.

Though no two childhoods are the same, three father types show up most often in father-wound stories—distant dads, disappointed dads, and destructive dads.

DISTANT DADS: A LACK OF PROXIMITY

Distant dads leave a child with a void where guidance, encouragement, and protection were meant to grow. My dad died when I was six. His absence wasn't his fault, but the ache remained. Other distant dads may be deployed, divorced, or just emotionally detached and unavailable—present in body but unreachable in heart. Some children grow up watching their distracted father pour time into work or hobbies but never into his child's forming heart. Others had strong, silent fathers who rarely showed affection, teaching without words that emotions were weak and help was a burden. As a result, these children often view God as similarly detached.

In contrast, God is the Father who never leaves. We hold His gaze and His delight as He lavishes love upon us. And in every space where we struggle or find our souls overwhelmed, He invites us to run to His throne of grace assured of His goodness (1 Peter 1:7).

DISAPPOINTED DADS: A LACK OF PRAISE

Disappointed dads rarely voice praise, pleasure, or pride in their children, and their silence becomes deafening. Whether they're disappointed in their child, themselves, or life in general, the result is the same. Kids of these dads feel they're a constant letdown. Some live under impossibly high standards. Others feel invisible in the shadow of a father's unhealed regret.

Children of disappointed dads tend to operate as perfectionists tying their worth to what they do. They believe they must get it right before they can be worthy of love, affection, or rest. They're prone to become people-pleasers, or break under pressure and simply lose heart. Their image of God is often a hard-to-please critic rather than a loving Father.

In contrast, Scripture reminds us that even when our hearts accuse us or try to shame us, God sees the full truth about us, and His fixed verdict carries greater authority than our ever-changing feelings (1 John 3:20). He welcomes us fully and delights in us as His beloved children. We're continually surrounded and saturated in the unending love of the Father. And we live in the staggering reality that, by the time we opened our eyes this morning, our Creator had already thought more thoughts about us than all the sand on the beaches in Hawaii (Psalm 139:17–18).

DESTRUCTIVE DADS: A LACK OF PROTECTION

Destructive dads are those who inflict harm on their children emotionally, verbally, physically, or sexually. This kind of abuse is the deepest betrayal, decimating a child's identity and sense of worth. The damage runs deep, often cloaked in secrecy and shame. These children grow up battling anxiety, addiction, or self-hatred, unsure why they struggle to believe in love at all. If a father's love was unsafe, God's love feels foreign. But our true Father is nothing like that. He rescues the weak and defends the wounded. He is the perfect love who casts out our every fear (1 John 4:18).

If any of the above is reminiscent of your experience with your earthly father, I offer some help in the healing process at the conclusion of this chapter. As I grieve with you in this moment, I also stand wildly expectant for the healing that waits as you embrace the Father you were created to know! Keep going. Hope is on the way.

SPIRITUAL FATHERLESSNESS

It should not surprise us that the patterns that shape our physical relationships with our fathers often echo in the spiritual relationships we form with those who have authority in the Church. The imprint of fathering does not stop at the threshold of the home. It often continues in how we view pastors, mentors, and leaders. And in turn, it silently sculpts our perception of God.

Children who feel unseen or unsafe with their spiritual leaders often struggle to believe God sees them or can be trusted. The wounds of spiritual authority gone wrong cut deep, not only because they harm, but because they do so in the name of the One who is meant to heal.

As you consider your story, take a moment to reflect on a few questions:

- What kind of God did your church speak of—one of invitation or one of interrogation?
- Were the leaders tender and trustworthy, or did they guard their position with distance or fear?
- Did you feel seen? Known? Or were you left to assume God's attention was reserved for those more spiritual, polished, or put together than you?
- Were words spoken, glances given, or tones used that quietly etched into your soul an image of a Father who was impossible to please?

Our early encounters with spiritual authority carry great weight because we believe these are the people God appointed to represent His heart. If those entrusted with shepherding souls misuse that trust, it could leave a scar not just toward the church, but toward God Himself. Where spiritual leaders were aloof or authoritarian, modeling a God who was angry, disappointed, or emotionally unpredictable, we often internalized this message. And over time, we began to confuse their voice with His.

WHAT I'M NOT SAYING

Before we continue, it's important to pause and say clearly what I am not saying.

This is not a call to point fingers at our fathers, mothers, or spiritual leaders and hold them solely responsible for our wounds. We live in a world that is both breathtakingly beautiful and tragically broken. None of us escape without scars. And none of us, me included, have parented or led without making mistakes.

A growing tendency in our culture villainizes authority and clings to victimhood. That's not the heart of this book. The cross of Christ does not just expose pain…it redeems it. It does not leave us bound in grief or blame. It offers us a path into healing, freedom, and restoration.

Yes, people have failed us, but they too often operate from places of deep personal pain that is still being healed. Hurting people hurt people. The brokenness they caused in our lives was merely a mirror of the brokenness they carried. And if we will not allow the Father to heal us, we will pass it on too.

This is why we must confront the truth about our stories—not to get stuck in them, but to be set free. The enemy has always sought to undermine the image of the Father in our earliest years. He tried to kill Moses as an infant. He tried to kill Jesus as an infant. And he knows if he can distort the Father's face while we are still learning to see, we'll spend our lives afraid to look again. But that's not where your story ends.

Please don't forget, many have loved you well—mothers and fathers, pastors and teachers, mentors and friends who showed up with fierce, faithful love. If their faces come to mind right now, take a moment to thank God for them. Maybe even reach out to thank them. And to every dad reading this, lift your head. Square your shoulders.

You've been entrusted with holy ground of the heart of your child. You don't have to get it all right. But your presence, your gaze, your blessing, your delight matters. It all reveals the Father. And you were created to carry that kind of love.

GETTING FREE OF THE ORPHAN SPIRIT

Fathers, mothers, and spiritual leaders shape our earliest conceptions of God as Father, and for many, these conceptions carry great pain and distance into adulthood. This is the key fruit of the orphan spirit. By this, I mean the universal propensity of mankind to believe we are on our own in the world, needing to protect ourselves, provide for our own welfare, and promote our own agenda in the world.

THREE S'S OF THE ORPHAN SPIRIT

The orphan spirit is undergirded by feelings of shame, blame, and fear. This spirit usually expresses itself in one of the three S's below.

Scarcity—There's not enough, so I must...
Striving—I'm not enough, so I must...
Scapegoating—You're not enough, so I must...

Orphanhood is a scheme our enemy has been pursuing for a long time. Leif Hetland put into words what is happening beneath the surface. "Many of humanity's problems can be traced back to the orphan spirit. It is an ancient spirit unleashed upon mankind through the work of the Evil One. It is a spirit whose chief joy is to separate children from their Father...his primary goal is to turn everyone into a version of himself—fatherless, disinherited, and lost."[3]

The following list is not exhaustive, and several of the responses can easily be categorized in multiple groupings. But this is a good start to help you recognize behaviors and responses rooted in an orphan mentality with God. They fall into the categories of fear, fight, and shame.

Fear-based responses

- Striving (Fear of Failure). "My performance determines my worth."
- Control (Fear of Danger). "I have to know or I have to be in charge to be at peace."
- Worry (Fear of Lack). "I have to figure out how to provide for myself."
- Religion (Fear of Judgment). "If I don't keep God's rules well enough, I'm in danger."
- Flattering Tongue/Dishonesty (Fear of Conflict). "I must tell you what you want to hear."
- Image/Appearance (Fear of Disapproval/Loneliness). "I must project myself as someone you will respect."
- Scapegoating (Fear of Injustice). "They must be shut down in order for us to be lifted up."

Fight-based responses

- Anger/Inability to Forgive/Resentment. "They have to make what they did right."
- Gossip/Division. "You need to know what they've done."
- Blame (God/Others). "They are the reason I am in pain."
- Jealousy. "I would be happy if I had what they have."

Shame-based responses

- Guilt. "If you only knew what I've done."
- Rejection. "I do not deserve to find love/friendship/community."
- Insecurity/Unworthiness. "I struggle to see why God or others

would love me."

- Doubt of God's Goodness or Promises. "I believe God moves for others, but not for me."
- Isolation/Difficulty trusting others. "God and people will ultimately let me down."
- Hopelessness/Despair. "I will always be in the pain I am in now."
- Restlessness. "Nothing will ever truly fulfill me."

As you read this list, which responses and behaviors stood out to you? Perhaps you saw several and got a little discouraged. But I beg you to see this truth through a new lens. Every item on the list above invites you, without condemnation, to experience a new revelation of who your Father truly is.

The universal human problem is the orphan spirit. And the universal invitation to be a child of God is found on a cross. This invitation is from the One who came to reveal who our Father has always been. Whatever you are tempted to feel in this moment, I promise at the center of it all lies this one fundamental truth about your heart. Your heart is crying out to be fathered.

HOPE FOR THE ORPHAN SPIRIT OF FEAR

"The Spirit you received does not make you slaves, so that you live in fear again; rather, the Spirit you received brought about your adoption to sonship. And by him we cry, 'Abba, Father.' The Spirit himself testifies with our spirit that we are God's children" (Romans 8:15–16 NIV).

Your spiritual adoption sent an eviction notice to fear and its right to operate in your life. And now, as you get to know God as Father, you can release the need to be your own provider, protector, and promoter, and just be His beloved.

HOPE FOR THE ORPHAN SPIRIT OF ANGER

"For we know that the whole creation has been groaning together in the pains of childbirth until now. And not only the creation, but we ourselves, who have the firstfruits of the Spirit, groan inwardly as we wait eagerly for adoption as sons" (Romans 8:22–23a).

We passionately yearn for everything broken to be made right, but that yearning isn't for vengeance. It's for adoption. It's a desire to know the Father of Justice has seen our cause, and He will bring the full inheritance He promised, even as we stand in confidence bearing the first fruits of His indwelling Spirit.

HOPE FOR THE ORPHAN SPIRIT OF SHAME

"See what great love the Father has lavished on us, that we should be called children of God! And that is what we are!...Dear friends, now we are children of God" (1 John 3:1–2 NIV).

"I am my beloved's and my beloved is mine" (Song of Solomon 6:3).

At the cross, God baptized you into His love. Imagine God's love like one of those giant buckets at a water park, completely overwhelming and drenching you. Today, He calls you His beloved. It means His favorite.[4] They say parents shouldn't play favorites. But our Father only plays favorites, and you, Beloved, will come to see sooner than you know that He loves you, and He likes you. In time, you will love and like you too.

Over the next chapters, we will walk through the story of the Bible to see how Jesus unveils the glorious picture of who the Father has always been. But before we move forward, would you pause and ask God where He is calling you to forgive? Ask Him where you need healing from wounds received in your childhood affecting how you see Him as Father.

Your Father delights in you and cannot wait to take you deeper into His Love. He came so you'd never be fatherless again.

DISCUSSION QUESTIONS

1. Which type of father wound (distant, disappointed, or destructive) has most shaped your story, and how has it influenced the way you see God?

2. Reflect on the spiritual leaders or church communities in your early faith journey. Did they model a God who was approachable, joyful, and loving, or one who was strict, silent, or angry?
3. Of the three S's of the orphan spirit (scarcity, striving, scapegoating), which one do you find yourself most tempted to live from?

TWO

MY TWO (SCHIZOPHRENIC) DADS

How the God of the Old Testament and the God of the New aren't at odds

FOR AS LONG AS I CAN REMEMBER, I've believed in the God of the Bible in a personal way. I don't have a dramatic conversion story. Simply put, I can't remember a time before knowing Jesus. That said, if heaven had a relationship status page, mine with God from childhood well into my early adult years would've read, "It's complicated."

I believed God was real. I believed He created the world, sustained it, and He performed miracles. I also believed He was personally involved in my life. That's what scared me. My earliest view of God was a lot like Santa Claus—*He sees you when you're sleeping...He knows if you've been bad or good.* But instead of coal, God held the threat of a lake of fire "where their worm does not die and the fire is not quenched" (Mark 9:48).

I didn't memorize the Bible, but I knew that one.

I didn't just pray once for salvation, I prayed it hundreds of times. More if you counted the times I stayed in my seat to pray because I was too embarrassed to go forward. I wasn't sure if that counted, though, or if it simply revealed I was one of those lukewarm people He'd warned about, but I digress.

At fifteen, I committed to reading through the Bible. That's when everything escalated. You know when you buy a new car and suddenly you see that particular car everywhere? They call it the Baader-Meinhof Phenomenon. That was me, with judgment. I couldn't read three verses without seeing God's anger, disappointment, or warnings about my deceitful heart. I saw judgment everywhere, even in passages I was reading way out of context.

At church, I found myself drifting in and out of listening, until a phrase would be spoken (or at several churches, shouted) that snapped me back to reality. I was a sinner. God was greatly displeased. This moment was my chance to fix it before He ran out of patience with me. Thank you, Reverend Baader-Meinhof, for once again reinforcing my worldview of terror.

Most days, I locked myself in my room to make myself read the Bible. A self-imposed prison sentence, attempting to dig out of my pit of shame one devotion at a time in my own spiritual *Shawshank Redemption.* When summer storms rolled in, I trembled. Surely this was God thundering His anger. I repented for everything—bad actions, bad thoughts about bad actions, even bad temptations about bad thoughts about bad actions. If I walked into a room and saw a pile of clothes on the floor, I feared I'd been left behind.

In all of this, I never thought God was the monster. I was convinced the true monster was me.

TWO ANGELS NAMED CHRIS

Two leaders stepped into my life who began to shift my view of God. Strangely, both were named Chris.

My siblings and I walked or rode bikes to a country church we called The Chapel, a small white building that smelled like mothballs and looked like Grandma's house. On Sunday nights, we returned for youth group where teens skated a giant halfpipe before a man named Chris Noble led a Bible study.

Chris was soft-spoken, patient, and gentle. A stark contrast to the fiery preacher from Sunday mornings. He smiled often and treated everyone with grace. Chris gave me my first Bible, with an inscription,

"Chuck, be the Bible, the whole Bible, and nothing but the Bible." I read this countless times. He saw me, and he believed I could live a life faithful to God's Word. It certainly made me double down my efforts to try. Though Chris Noble was only in my life a few years, I will forever thank God for him.

Years later, in my senior year of high school, a persistent group of friends finally convinced me to join them for a weekend youth retreat. Nervous, I followed them into a room packed with teenagers. An overly energetic guy sat behind us. They all seemed to know him, and he really focused on keeping our attention by trying to make a joke out of everything. If you've ever seen Robin Williams on a late-night show, you get the idea. I was pretty sure this kid was held back a few years, as he looked to be a young adult still hanging out with us teens. I thought maybe his parents sent him, hoping we'd help him become socially adjusted. I smiled awkwardly at him. When we got back to the room, they introduced him as the youth pastor they told me about, a man named Chris Thomas! Imagine my surprise.

Intrigued, I visited church the next week and saw a completely different dimension to this man. He led worship with passion and tenderness. He taught the Bible in a way that made it come alive. Chris didn't just preach like God loved us; he was convinced that God liked us too. That was new for me. His sermons weren't threats to outrun but invitations to draw close.

I began volunteering at church and Chris welcomed me into his life. He taught me, quoted dumb movie lines with me, gave me lots of advice, and believed in me. He was unorthodox, for sure. Once, suspecting I thought food had to be prayed over before God blessed it, Chris popped a fry into his mouth after we left a drive-thru and smiled at me. When I protested that we had to pray, he looked at me and said, "Jesus, thank you. Amen." Eyes open and everything. Over time, his irreligious freedom began to erode my fear and introduce me to a God of joy.

Later that summer, at a camp in Georgia, I finally mustered the strength to tell Chris about a long-hidden addiction. I was sure this would be the end of my place in the church. Chris listened. He never looked shocked or disappointed. Not once. With conviction, he affirmed the love for God he saw in my heart. He told me how proud he was of me, and he committed to meet with me regularly until this addiction was a part of my past. And that's exactly what he did. Today, Chris is my closest friend, in every sense my brother, and a fellow pastor at our home church. Through the past quarter of a century, God has used Chris Thomas continually to lead me deeper into His compassion, His joy, and His faithfulness.

Two angels named Chris helped anchor my warring soul. Still, much of my early faith felt like spiritual pinball, bouncing between security and shame. How could I grow up surrounded by churches, Christians, and the Bible, and still encounter two drastically different pictures of God? As I've learned, I'm not alone. Sometimes, even within Scripture, God appears as two very different characters.

GOD BEHAVING BEAUTIFULLY

Consider these precious promises…

- "God is love…there is no fear in love" (1 John 4:16b, 18a).
- "God is light, and in him is no darkness at all" (1 John 1:5b).
- "Oh give thanks to the Lord, for He is good; for his steadfast love endures forever!" (1 Chronicles 16:34).
- "The Lord, the Lord, the compassionate and gracious God, slow to anger, abounding in love and faithfulness" (Exodus 34:6 NIV).
- "The Lord loves righteousness and justice; the earth is full of his unfailing love" (Psalm 33:5 NIV).
- "He will take great delight in you; in his love he will no longer rebuke you, but will rejoice over you with singing" (Zephaniah 3:17b NIV).

God is love. He cannot act apart from it. God is light. He is not party to darkness. God is good, just, powerful, and entirely present. He cannot be manipulated or corrupted. And though He possesses unlimited strength, God chooses intimacy. The same hand that ordered the cosmos cradles your heart with tender care.

This is the image of a God behaving beautifully.

GOD BEHAVING BADLY?

But then…the other image exists too. One less like joy and happiness and more like Jekyll and Hyde. Consider this…

- "In the Old Testament, God seems to command Israel to wipe out entire nations, including women, children, and animals."[5]
- He floods the earth, sparing one family and a zoo. (See Genesis 7)
- He incinerates a city and turns a woman to salt. (See Genesis 19)
- One day, Moses calls for the execution of 3,000 Israelites, saying God blessed them to carry it out. (See Exodus 32:29)
- God strikes Uzzah for steadying the Ark. (See 2 Samuel 6:6–7)
- He sends fire from heaven at Elijah's request, which Elijah took as a mandate to slaughter 450 false prophets. (See 1 Kings 18)

To many modern readers, these truths feel like spiritual whiplash.

Is this the same loving God? How do these acts differ from the blood-stained atrocities we've seen carried out for centuries in the name of religion? Is ours okay because it takes place in our holy book and not someone else's? More deeply, how do we trust a Father who seems so volatile? What seems to be a contradictory image of God has led some to reject the possibility of God altogether.

Evolutionary biologist and author Richard Dawkins is one of the most outspoken critics of Christianity and religion, particularly in the portrayal of God presented in the Old Testament. Dawkins describes God as "arguably the most unpleasant character in all fiction: jealous and proud of it; a petty, unjust, unforgiving control-freak; a vindictive, bloodthirsty, ethnic cleanser; a misogynistic, homophobic, racist, infanticidal, genocidal, filicidal, pestilential, megalomaniacal, sadomasochistic, capriciously malevolent bully."[6]

I bet he is fun at dinner parties. (Yeesh!)

It's easy to be defensive and label someone like Dawkins as miserable, mean, or worse. It's far more responsible to patiently consider his statement, refuse to submerge uncomfortable passages about God into a sea of ignorance, and choose the courage to honestly wrestle with them. What most frustrates Dawkins and many intellectual atheists like him is how little Christians know about troubling descriptions of God *in their own Bible.*

We cannot blissfully ignore these questions. It's not because we need an answer for our critics, but because somewhere, in the recesses of our own minds, in the places we haven't formulated into words, we wrestle with the fear that God is not as good as He promised. Every fear, worry, doubt, and attempt to control our surroundings proves this wrestling with the true nature of our Father.

But I believe something greater than the mantra "God is good." I believe God is Goodness itself. He is not merely loving. God is love, running wider and longer and higher and deeper than the furthest reach of our imagination or understanding (Ephesians 3:19–20). But we will not encounter His goodness and love if we try to keep a vilified version of Him subdued in the cellar of our souls. We must wrestle with it.

TRUSTING THE GOD OF THE BIBLE

So, what do we do with these troubling passages?

Some respond by abandoning a traditional view of biblical inspiration. They try to embrace what the Bible says about Jesus while distancing themselves from much of the Old Testament. But Jesus Himself affirmed the Old Testament and said He came to fulfill it.

"Do not think that I have come to abolish the Law or the Prophets; I have not come to abolish them but to fulfill them. For truly, I say to you, until heaven and earth pass away, not an iota, not a dot, will pass from the Law until all is accomplished" (Matthew 5:17–18).

The conditional acceptance of truth is troubling because all the truths we claim find their origin in the Bible. If we distrust portions of it, how can we be certain about any of it? Who decides what's true and what isn't? If the foundation is shaky, the house we build can't stand.

My greatest concern with this partial inspiration approach is it places us, not God, in the editor's seat. The Bible becomes a rough draft we trim and highlight according to our preferences. Like a modern return to Babel, we construct towers of our own ideas that impress us so greatly, we convince ourselves God is blessing them. But just as in Babel, we cannot see the great deception and confusion among us.

Some communicators hold to the inspiration of the Bible but go to great lengths to sanitize it, polishing every passage until it feels neat, tidy, and emotionally manageable. They speak in sweeping but generic terms about God's love, grace, and acceptance in sentiments that rival a Hallmark card. But they fail to wrestle with deeper questions about justice, wrath, or pain.

Others react like children throwing a theological tantrum, slamming their fist on the table and shouting at anyone who fails to read it like they do. They don't engage in difficult passages with humility or patience. They simply name-call, manipulate, and accuse.

Still others approach the Bible like forensic analysts at a crime scene, working overtime to erase any trace of God's fingerprints from difficult passages. They propose the authors were mistaken, reach for hyper-allegory, or insert their own conclusions into the text, shaping the story to match what they already decided must be true.

But there is another way.

As we'll explore in chapter 6, majesty and mystery fill Scripture by design. Like Job, we are invited to sit in the tension, to wrestle with questions we won't resolve on this side of heaven. That's not a flaw in the system—it's an attribute of God whose greatness no mind can fully contain.

He is the God of all science. But endless expressions of quantum physics, cosmology, biology, and astrophysics revolve in our ever-expanding universe. We quite simply lack the capacity to perceive, explain, or comprehend these. And that's okay. For a little perspective, it is believed we can only observe about four percent of the created universe even with our best telescopes, satellites, and research. And that four percent has baffled even the most dedicated and brilliant thinkers in the human race.[7] Truth doesn't require our agreement to be true.

Majesty and mystery remain, and no attempt is made in this book to remove either, as I believe they are a gift from God. God is God, and He is overwhelmingly good, even when, especially when, we fail to perceive it.

Beyond that, Scripture tells a singular, sweeping story—one many miss by focusing only on select verses, doctrines, or systems. We often work so hard to master the Bible, we miss the Master Himself.

God's Word is fully inspired by Him for the story He is trying to tell us. But we have a nagging historical habit of missing the point. We would be wise to realize one significant truth: The Bible is inspired. Our interpretation of it is not.

What if the Bible was never meant to be an encyclopedia to dissect? What if it's a window into the heart of a Father who has been revealing Himself all along, culminating in the person of Jesus?

That's where we're headed.

In the pages ahead, we will see how the whole story, from beginning to end, reveals who God is, and how God chose to reveal Himself through Jesus (Galatians 4:4–5). Jesus is the reflection of the Father without ambiguity. The whole story has always been about Him. It reveals His love for the human race and His great passion for us to walk in intimacy with Him once again.

It's a story of invitation and fierce rescue. It faithfully shares the reform plans we have attempted and the systems we have built in vain attempts to save ourselves, and the narrative shows us why they all ultimately fail. But mostly, this story urges us to come home to a really good Father whose arms are always open and whose gates are never shut.

In the end, we will see how our Father grants us the dignity to decide for ourselves whether we will return His gaze or look away, though He pursues our hearts relentlessly, even now. I only pray to be a faithful friend, sharing how my faith was transformed from wrestling into resting as I saw that God, my Father is no schizophrenic. He has always looked like Jesus.

DISCUSSION QUESTIONS

1. Have you felt tension between the God you read about in parts of the Bible and the God revealed in Jesus? How has that shaped the way you trust, or struggle to trust, God's heart?
2. Which view of Scripture do you find yourself leaning toward: trying to sanitize the hard parts, avoiding them altogether, or facing them honestly but cautiously?
3. "The Bible is inspired. Our interpretation of it is not." How does this truth invite you to hold your conclusions with humility and remain open to seeing God more clearly through Scripture?

THREE

DAD LOOKS JUST LIKE JESUS

Seeing the Cross at the center of everything

MY WIFE JILL AND I LOVE WATCHING true crime shows. Weird, I know. But the mystery, the pursuit of truth, and the hope of justice draw us in. That said, I'd make a terrible detective. With every new suspect, I'm quick to shout, "Guilty!" at the screen only to change my theory after the next commercial break. We're quick to build stories from fragments, often mistaking pieces for the whole. Take the case of Michael Morton.

August 1986. Texas.

Michael and Christine Morton had been married for seven years. Their three-year-old son Eric had just recovered from open-heart surgery, and the emotional toll of parenting a medically fragile child strained their marriage. Michael shared with friends he no longer felt pursued by his wife. Still, they were known to resolve their disagreements quickly.

The day after Michael's thirty-second birthday, Christine was found beaten to death in their bed. Michael was at work. A neighbor saw Eric playing outside alone, and upon checking the house, discovered Christine.

Police found a note from Michael expressing deep frustration that, on the evening of his birthday, he felt slighted by his wife. Nonetheless, it closed with the words, "I love you." There were no signs of forced entry, no valuables stolen. But the scene looked staged and investigators grew suspicious.

Michael's lack of visible emotion and his choice to sleep in his home that night raised further questions. When the medical examiner estimated Christine's death at 1:30 a.m., five hours before Michael left for work, prosecutors had their story. Angry husband murders wife.

Michael was convicted and sentenced to life in prison.

For the next twenty-four years, Michael watched nearly everyone, his wife's family, his friends, even his son come to believe he was guilty. Eric stopped visiting at age fifteen. The court offered Michael parole if he showed remorse, but he answered firmly, "All I have left is my actual innocence. And if I have to be in prison the rest of my life, I'm not giving that up."[8]

Years later, The Innocence Project took his case. What they discovered was staggering. Fingerprints on the sliding glass door from the morning of the crime didn't match Michael or anyone in the home.

The medical examiner's time of death was only speculation and was misquoted to make it sound like a scientific conclusion. This had been the lynchpin in the case.

In a taped interview, Eric described a "monster with a mustache," stating his dad was not present. Little Eric claimed, "Only Mommy and Eric was there."

Most shocking of all, a bloodstained bandana was discovered in the backyard and held in evidence. But they never tested it or admitted this evidence in the trial. The jury never knew it existed.

DNA on the bandana matched both Christine and a man named Mark Alan Norwood. Norwood was a drifter with a violent past, including an arrest for the murder of another woman two years after Christine's. That murder matched the modus operandi and crime scene precisely.

Michael Morton had been framed, sentenced, and forgotten. But he was innocent. From behind bars, he earned degrees in psychology and literature, and he found God before he was ultimately exonerated. Reflecting on his life today, Michael shared, "I know three simple things. One, God exists. Two, He is wise. He's smarter than I am. And three, He loves me. Once you know those three things, what's your problem?"[9]

The beauty of Michael Morton's redemption, humility, and vindication is breathtaking. But we must wonder how the truth, sitting in plain daylight, could be overlooked for an alternate narrative that turned an innocent man into a monster. The answer is simple. If we don't know what the story is about, we will make it about something else.

The police thought they knew the story. Jilted husband attacks wife. So, they used the details they found to match their narrative and discarded the rest. We do the same with the Bible. We cherry-pick verses and fill in the gaps to fit whatever narrative we've already come to suspect. And for countless people reading the Bible through the lens of childhood father-wounds, the troubling passages of the Old Testament provide all the evidence needed to convict God of criminal neglect and abuse. Those of us who see God that way need a new lens. Jesus met two grieving sons on the road to do just that.

THE EMMAUS LENS

Two men walked along the road trying to piece together the past days' broken fragments. As worshippers of God, they were confident they knew where the story was headed. But all of that changed on a Friday. As they walked, they talked about the prophet named Jesus who'd appeared in their midst, and how for the last three years He altered reality beyond anything they'd believed possible.

He healed the sick, cleansed lepers, raised the dead, and forgave sin. When He spoke, the kingdom of God felt accessible and present. And perhaps the most miraculous of all was how He made them feel. They felt seen by Him and known and loved. They so hoped He would be the One to restore Israel.

But Jesus had been brutally executed. They watched as His lifeless body was carried into a tomb, sighing in resignation as the giant stone hid Him and hope from their eyes. All at once, their dreams dissipated like the dust they kicked up under their feet. Two men walked along the road trying to piece together the broken fragments. And they would have remained stuck there had a third man not joined them on the road.

This story in Luke 24 of Jesus walking incognito on the road to Emmaus with His confused kids, is a brilliant picture of what He's still doing today. The Holy God of Eternity chose incarnation to be with us on the road we're traveling in order to open our eyes to His glorious plan. Pay careful attention to what Luke wrote, "And beginning with Moses and all the Prophets, he interpreted to them in all the Scriptures the things concerning himself" (Luke 24:27).

God chose to progressively reveal His nature to His children in the pages of the Old Testament, through veils and shadows. But in the fullness of time, God sent Jesus who was the unveiling of who the Father has always been.

In this chapter, we will share four interpretive keys to frame our understanding of the Bible. As we do, we will quickly see how all the evidence points to a God who has never been guilty of the crimes our consciences have charged Him with. He has always and only been good.

Four simple truths help us see this clearly.

1. Jesus is the perfect reflection of the Father.
2. The whole story of the Bible is about Jesus and only makes sense through the lens of Jesus.
3. God is unchanging. Who Jesus is, the Father has always been.
4. How the Father approaches, loves, judges, and feels about people looks exactly like Jesus.

THE PERFECT REFLECTION OF THE FATHER

Near the end of His ministry, Jesus sat with His disciples after washing their feet. He had spoken of His death in metaphors like a kernel of wheat falling to the ground that produces many seeds (John 12:24). They were perplexed. Everything they learned about the coming kingdom looked like triumph, a victory lap, not a Via Dolorosa. But in John 14, Jesus leaned in to comfort His disciples with a different metaphor using the language of a wedding. It's important we understand how marriage operated in the Jewish culture.

A Jewish marriage had three stages. It began with a price, was sealed with a pledge, and then was fulfilled in permanence. The groom would pay a price for the bride, then pledge his vow before witnesses to take her as his wife. This legally made them husband and wife. But a third part of their union included the groom's departure to go prepare a permanent home, worthy to raise their family in. The bride never knew exactly when the groom would return, but the price and pledge assured her that permanence with him would be her inheritance. And so, Jesus told them, "I go to prepare a place for you," promising He would take them to be with Him and the Father forever (John 14:3). But instead of comfort, the disciples were confused.

"'If you had known me, you would have known my Father also. From now on you do know him and have seen him.' Philip said to him, 'Lord, show us the Father, and it is enough for us.' Jesus said to him, 'Have I been with you so long, and you still do not know me, Philip? Whoever has seen me has seen the Father. How can you say, "Show us the Father"?'" (John 14:7–9).

To the disciples, this would have seemed absolutely nuts. After all, Jesus was attempting to assure them of an experience for which they had no memory. The word *see* here in Greek means, to experience with the mind.[10] The word *know* means to encounter through firsthand experience.[11]

They had already *experienced* the Father? How could this be?

Undeterred, Philip pressed deeper asking Jesus to *show* Him the Father, or to "place him on exhibit."[12] If you've ever been to a science fair, you get the idea of what this means. Philip was saying, "No. Put Him on display. Let us literally see and touch the Father and discover how He works."

Keep in mind, the Israelites had a rich history of encountering the Father's presence in miraculous and undeniable ways. They saw Him many times in a cloud (see Exodus 24:16–18; Exodus 33:9; 1 Kings 8:10–13). God led them at night as a pillar of fire (Exodus 13:21–22). Moses' first encounter with God was Jehovah as a burning bush. Moses longed to see the Father even clearer but was told that no man can see God's face and live (Exodus 33:18–20). Thus, Philip's request wasn't just bold. It was an impossible inquiry met with a far more impossible answer.

Jesus said in effect, "Look in my eyes, Philip. If you've seen me, you've already seen the Father...and lived!"

Not a reflection. Not a personification. Not the closest compromise humanity could handle. No. "If you have seen me, you have seen the Father." Period.

Hebrews 1:3 NIV says, "The Son [Jesus] is the radiance of God's glory and the exact representation of his being." The Old Testament gives shadowed, veiled glimpses of God's glory. But Jesus is the full substance of the Father, in all His glory.[13]

Today, it's popular to post Instagram photos intended to show one's natural beauty with the tag #nofilter. Jesus is the Father #nofilter. If you want to know exactly who God the Father is, He isn't seen most clearly through the smoke of Sinai, but the smile of the Savior. Jesus is not merely similar to the Father. He is the exact representation of the Father's very being, down to every last detail.

That's why, when we read the Old Testament, we must let Jesus bring the shadows into focus. When we encounter veiled images of the Father in the pages, we look to Jesus to offer clarity on God's true nature.

And if ever the evidence we think we see does not match Jesus, we trust the substance of Jesus over our interpretation of the shadow. Remember, the Bible is inspired. Our interpretation is not. And Jesus is the key to our interpretation. I especially love how The Passion Translation expresses Hebrews 1:2. It says, "To us living in these last days, God now speaks to us openly in the language of a Son."

Jesus is the language the Father is speaking.

Paul wrote in Colossians 1:15 NIV, "The Son is the image of the invisible God." So, we can see and hear God by knowing Jesus, but it gets even better.

When a ruler came to power in biblical times, new currency was minted as the authorized way to buy, sell, and trade according to the law. That currency bore the image of the one who had been authorized to rule over that land. In the same way, Jesus is the Father's authoritative image through whom all kingdom commerce flows. The unchanging God will not redeem, bless, or exchange anything that does not bear the face of His Son.

Nonetheless, it's still far too popular a practice for people to use the shadow of Old Testament to try to argue with Jesus, somehow attempting to elevate the tablets of Mt. Sinai above the Teacher at the Sermon on the Mount.

God is one. He is not divided. And He didn't merely give us Jesus as another voice to throw into our biblical blenders alongside the actions of Moses and Elijah. They are the shadow. Jesus is the substance. We interpret all they said and did through Him, not the other way around, because Jesus is not simply a sincere image of the Father. He stands as the only sufficient one.

"For the entire fullness of God's nature dwells bodily in Christ, and you have been filled by him, who is the head over every ruler and authority" (Colossians 2:9–10 CSB).

The entire fullness of everything the Father is, thinks, and does is found in Jesus. He is the sufficient final word on all matters concerning the Father. Jesus is the Father with skin on, or in the words of A.M. Ramsey, "God is Christlike, and in him is no un-Christlikeness at all."[14]

THE WORD WHO UNLOCKS THE WORD

Jesus isn't just the key to understanding the Father. He's also the key who unlocks the Bible. We can only understand the written Word rightly by seeing the Living Word clearly. Scripture after Scripture celebrates this paramount truth.

- Jesus is the Word of God who came to dwell among us. (John 1:1, 1:14)
- The Bible is the Spirit-inspired Word that testifies to Him. (2 Timothy 3:16, Luke 24:27)
- Jesus is the living Word who is sharper than any two-edged sword, separating between our souls and spirits to show us the motives of our hearts (Hebrews 4:12).
- The Bible is the "more sure word of prophecy" that invites us to experience Jesus (2 Peter 1:19 KJV).

Scripture always points to Jesus. Beware of any teacher who loves to quote the written Word, but whose actions don't reveal the tender affection of the Living Word. This leader will use the sword of the Spirit, not as a surgeon's scalpel to heal, but as a weapon to assault the very ones Jesus drew near to save. Everything we encounter in the Bible leads us to love Jesus—and to love like Jesus. In Matthew 11, Jesus reveals a stunning truth about how the Father makes Himself known.

"You have hidden these things [the truths of your kingdom] from the wise and understanding and revealed them to little children...No one knows the Father except the Son and anyone to whom the Son chooses to reveal him" (Matthew 11:25, 27).

Jesus reveals the Father by offering Himself. And all we need to experience Him is to come to Him like a child. On the road to Emmaus, the fullness of the Father drew near to His kids to reteach the story.

"Beginning with Moses and all the Prophets, he interpreted to them in all the Scriptures the things concerning himself" (Luke 24:27). Luke continues the account with these words, "He said to them, 'Everything written about me in the Law of Moses and the Prophets and the Psalms must be fulfilled.' Then he opened their minds to understand the Scriptures" (Luke 24:44–45).

The disciples had devoted their lives to God. They loved Scripture. And still, they missed the plot. Why? Because they read the story without understanding, and the key to full revelation of God's glorious plan is Christ.

When Jesus mentioned the Law of Moses, the Prophets, and the Psalms, He was referring to the entire Old Testament. By including all three, He stated emphatically that the entire narrative was about Him, the uncovered reflection of the Father...and they had largely missed it.

Remember, if we don't know what God's story is about, *we will make it about something else.* So, many of them turned the story into a manual of moral law, imagining they could earn God's blessing through effort.

After beginning with such purity, the people traded their place in the global invitation to redemption for a license to elevate themselves above the rest of the world as God's chosen. They wrapped their exclusion in the language of holiness, called their self-protection devotion, and built walls in the very places God longed to come near to remove them. They strayed so far in pursuing their so-called Manifest Destiny, they no longer recognized the One they claimed to worship, even as He stood in front of them.

Consider the religious leaders of Jesus' day. They so misunderstood the story, they crucified the tangible image of the God they claimed to serve. It wasn't merely that they failed to recognize their Father. No. They condemned Jesus as a *son of the devil* (Matthew 12:24). In an age when many still interpret the biblical story through the same lens of conquest and empire that failed the Pharisees, this should shake us to a place of humble introspection.

Jesus made the point again in John 5. "You study the Scriptures diligently because you think that in them you have eternal life. These are the very Scriptures that testify about me" (John 5:39 NIV). Paul echoed Jesus' words when he later wrote, "I decided to know nothing among you except Jesus Christ and him crucified" (1 Corinthians 2:2).

In his next letter, Paul took the idea even further.

"Therefore, since we have such a hope, we are very bold. We are not like Moses, who would put a veil over his face to prevent the Israelites from seeing the end of what was passing away. But their minds were made dull, for to this day the same veil remains when the old covenant is read. It has not been removed, because only in Christ is it taken away. Even to this day when Moses is read, a veil covers their hearts. But whenever anyone turns to the Lord, the veil is taken away. Now the Lord is the Spirit, and where the Spirit of the Lord is, there is freedom. And we all, who with unveiled faces contemplate the Lord's glory, are being transformed into his image with ever-increasing glory, which comes from the Lord, who is the Spirit" (2 Corinthians 3:12–18 NIV).

It's possible to love the Word of God, to highlight it, memorize it, and tweet about it, and still not get it. The veil, which keeps us from fully seeing His glory, is only removed when we see through the lens of Christ. We experience freedom as our uncovered faces look upon the radiant face of God in Christ. Hallelujah!

And consider this. Just as your shadow faithfully renders the outline of your body, yet distorts its appearance based on where the light illumines it, the Old Testament is the fully inspired Word about Jesus that comes as a shadow at various times throughout the day of revelation. The Word is true, but without standing at its source, we can project a wildly distorted image in our imagination.

If you've ever thought the shadow of the shirt hanging in your closet was an intruder waiting to kill you, you know what I mean. (I probably need to stop watching so many crime shows.)

The Old Testament is the story of our fall and our wrestling between kingdoms. It reveals God's relentless pursuit, and ultimately His appearance from the shadow realm into the substance named Jesus.

The law is only a shadow of the good things that are coming—not the realities themselves. Jesus is the reality! The Old Testament always pointed forward to a Person. We read Scripture through Jesus. He is the Word who unlocks the Word.

UNCHANGEABLE GOD

"You, Lord, laid the foundations of the earth in the beginning, and the heavens are the work of your hands; they will perish...but you are the same, and your years will have no end" (Hebrews 1:10, 12b).

"Jesus Christ is the same yesterday and today and forever" (Hebrews 13:8).

Stated another way, God always looks like Himself. If you see one snapshot of Jesus, you know who your Father has always been. James echoed this truth. "Every gift God freely gives us is good and perfect, streaming down from the Father of lights, who shines from the heavens with no hidden shadow or darkness and is never subject to change" (James 1:17 TPT).

God does not change. Who He was in the first page of the Bible, He is at the end of time. But though God remains the same, our perception of Him does not. Just as shadows change shape depending on our position to the light, our understanding of God becomes distorted when we lose sight of Jesus, the true radiance of the Father. The closer we move toward Him, the clearer God's face becomes.

God never changes His mind. His will, His delight, His ways are unshakable (Hebrews 6:17). God didn't suddenly get angry at sin one day and choose to wipe out humanity as His Plan A, scurrying anxiously to secure a Plan B. No.

"The Lamb who was slain from the creation of the world" (Revelation 13:8b NIV).

"His works were finished from the foundation of the world" (Hebrews 4:3).

Any emotionally abrupt language in the text was given for our benefit to understand the dire nature of our sin, our urgent need for rescue, and His unending love. His love would stop at nothing to bring us home. Who Jesus is, the Father has always been. And He can be trusted.

LIKE FATHER, LIKE SON

We must remember the truth about Jesus.

- Jesus is the perfect reflection of the Father. #nofilter
- The Bible only makes sense through the lens of Jesus.
- Who Jesus is, the Father has always been.

All of this leads us to one final life-altering truth—that the Father approaches humanity exactly how Jesus did.

God inspired all Scripture, but it's not all equally clear or profitable. I'll prove it to you. Many people tattoo *I can do all things through him who gives me strength* (see Phillippians 4:13) on their arms as a life mantra.

Meanwhile, considerably fewer people have opted for this gem.

"As part of your equipment have something to dig with, and when you relieve yourself, dig a hole and cover up your excrement" (Deuteronomy 23:13 NIV).

Both are inspired Scriptures. They are not, however, equally profitable. And they don't both reveal the heart of God or what He is up to on earth. Jesus is our interpretive lens. When the Old Testament says one thing and Jesus says another, as He did on the Sermon on the Mount, we don't treat Jesus' words as a footnote but take our cue from Him. He is not one biblical voice among many. He is *the* voice to which all the others were pointing.

So, how does the Father approach lawbreakers and the broken? Jesus shows us.

Exhibit A: The Woman Caught in Adultery (John 8)

Dragged into the public square by religious leaders quoting chapter and verse, the woman caught in adultery had far more than her shame to worry about. "'In the Law, Moses commanded us to stone such a woman'" (John 8:5).

And they knew chapter and verse to back it up.

"If a man is found sleeping with another man's wife, both the man who slept with her and the woman must die. You must purge the evil from Israel. If a man happens to meet in a town a virgin pledged to be married and he sleeps with her, you shall take both of them to the gate of that town and stone them to death" (Deuteronomy 22:22–24 NIV).

Other than the obvious fact that they omitted holding the man accountable, they had proof to back up their protest. They were purging the evil among them in the name of the Lord. The lines were drawn in black and white, *inspired by God,* showing that the Father demanded such a woman to die a bloody, public death for her shameless pursuit of immorality. The Law said it. And so, they asked Jesus, "What do you say?" (John 8:5 NIV).

But Jesus bent down and refused to answer. Instead, He began writing in the sand. Some scholars believe He wrote a message of hope to the woman. Finally, Jesus stood and told them the only one with the right to judge her would be one without sin.

One by one, they left. But don't miss this. One was present who never sinned, and He defied their understanding of the Law of Moses, doing precisely the opposite of what the Law required. He did not condemn her. Instead, He invited her to leave her life of missing the mark behind her. *And the Father has always been exactly like Jesus.*

Exhibit B: The Samaritan Woman (John 4)

Jesus and His disciples were headed to Galilee, and interestingly, the text says He *had* to go through Samaria (John 4:4). However, Jewish travelers had established an alternate route around Samaria precisely to avoid any contact with a people they considered half-breeds. By this point in history, this detour was the expected road, especially for a rabbi. The necessity Jesus felt wasn't about a map. It was about a mission.

He sent His disciples to buy food and sat upon Jacob's famous well. At the hottest point of the day, a Samaritan woman came alone to draw water. This was a red flag for two reasons. First, women traveled together to draw water, for protection and the camaraderie of community. (I am guessing this was their version of going to the bathroom together). A woman coming to the well alone was unusual. Secondly, this was the hottest point of the day. This woman arrived at a time she knew she wouldn't encounter anyone.

But as she approached, Jesus was waiting for her. He asked for a drink, which shocked her because Jews and Samaritans didn't talk to each other. He said He came to give her *living water.* When she questioned His ability to deliver on such a lavish promise, Jesus revealed that he knew everything about her.

He knew she had been married five times and currently lived with a man who was not her husband. Yet Jesus hadn't come to correct or condemn her. He came to sit with her and offer a way out of her soul's drought. Elated, she left her social exile to tell everyone about the God who had seen her. Jesus chose a foreign woman from a despised lineage and a checkered past to become the first missionary to lead an entire town to His feet. *And the Father has always been exactly like Jesus.*

Exhibit C: Tax Collectors and Sinners (Matthew 9)

Cultural traitors and moral outcasts, tax collectors, were fellow Jews who made a deal with Rome to take money from their own people, often at great profit for themselves. Sinners were those guilty of any number of lifestyle choices deemed unworthy by the respected members of society, treated as spiritual failures by the religious elite. Today, they would be found among LGBTQ+ communities, sex offenders, alcoholics, and the homeless, to name a few.

Jesus drew sharp criticism from the religious leaders, who were armed with verses about hating the company of evil people and refusing to sit with the wicked (Psalm 26:5). On one of these occasions, Jesus answered plainly, "It is not the healthy who need a doctor, but the sick. But go and learn what this means: 'I desire mercy, not sacrifice.' For I have not come to call the righteous, but sinners" (Matthew 9:12–13 NIV).

The religious leaders wanted hell, but Jesus responded with a hospital. They wanted a trial, but Jesus chose a table. *And the Father has always been exactly like Jesus.*

Jesus is the full, unchanging reflection of the Father. We must step out of the shadows of fear, legalism, and distorted theology to see clearly. The Father is no monster in a closet. *Dad has always and only looked just like Jesus.*

DISCUSSION QUESTIONS

1. How does the story of Michael Morton challenge the way we approach the Bible or form conclusions about God's character?
2. How might your relationship with God change if you fully believe the Father is exactly like Jesus in mercy, grace, and justice?
3. What does it look like in today's culture to welcome modern-day outcasts as Jesus did? Are there groups or individuals you struggle to see through the lens of Jesus' compassion?

FOUR

"HOLD WHAT YOU'VE GOT."

Starting from the beautiful strands of the gospel we already see

SOME OF MY FONDEST MEMORIES from childhood were summers spent with my grandparents in South Carolina. Every year, my sister and I packed up for the Lake House, where my Nana and Papa treated us like royalty.

Mornings greeted us with the smell of sizzling bacon and eggs, almost carrying us to the table where a feast awaited. Outside, acres of lakefront property stretched out before us, inviting us into endless adventure.

But my favorite moments were spent out in the boat with my Papa. He taught me how to drive at a young age, giving me the thrill of opening the engine wide across the glassy waters.

Papa went home to be with the Lord recently, but I can still hear his voice echo in my heart—words he must have said a thousand times when we were on the water. Wherever I got it right, or just needed a little reassurance, he would smile at me and say, "That's good, boy. Hold what you've got."

That simple phrase (part affection, part blessing) still steadies me. And I think it's exactly the kind of counsel we need for the waters we're navigating now.

Up to this point, we've talked about the need to ask vulnerable, honest questions about our faith. But if we're not careful, all that questioning can cause us to fear that everything we've learned is mistaken, that our faith needs to be gutted and rebuilt from scratch. We can become like Peter, asking Jesus for the full bucket shower from *Flashdance*, when we're already clean and simply need our feet washed to walk the path ahead of us.

Here's the truth. While we have areas requiring our continual rethinking and realigning to hold a faith worthy of the gospel, so many things we've learned in our faith journey need to be affirmed and celebrated. You and I have believed many things correctly, like strands of a tapestry God has been knitting for many years.

Before we dive into the Old Testament in the next chapter to challenge some long-held theological assumptions, let's pause. Let's anchor our hearts in the security of His love. If we look up, we will see the sail carrying our vessel is the very tapestry we invited the Father to keep expanding before our eyes.

And, if we close our eyes and listen closely, we might feel the breeze brush our face as we hear the delight of our Father whispering, *That's good. Hold what you've got!*

GETTING OUR BEARINGS

If you're reading this book and haven't yet read through the entire Bible, I want to offer some encouragement at the outset. While we'll wrestle with some difficult passages, the overwhelming majority of how God is revealed in the Old Testament is immediately beautiful, deeply compelling, and wholly consistent with what we see in Jesus of Nazareth.

His character, His calls to our hearts, and His invitation to partner with Him have been present from the very beginning—woven like golden threads through every generation of the story.

Three threads help us get our bearings.

- God's Character: Who He is.
- God's Commandment: What He desires us to be.
- God's Commission: How He chooses to work through us.

When we keep these in view, we'll see that even in the hardest passages, our faithful God is there, inviting us to walk with Him.

GOD'S CHARACTER: WHO HE IS

On Mt. Sinai, Moses drew near to God to receive the Law that would govern the people of Israel, but he wanted more than mere precepts about God. He needed to encounter God's presence.

So, Moses boldly declared, "Please show me your glory" (Exodus 33:18). In response, God hid Moses in the cleft of the rock and passed by him in radiant power. Moses saw only God's back, but the experience transformed him, sending him back to the people like a human Lite-Brite for weeks to come. What Moses heard when God passed by would become the Father's most repeated self-revelation in the Old Testament, quoted or alluded to 185 times.

Allow me to put that in perspective. My legal name is Charles, but no one who truly knows me calls me that. They call me Chuck. If you followed me around as a kid, you'd hear me politely correct rosters, introductions, and doctor's appointments with the request, "Please call me Chuck." This moment on Sinai was God's, "Please call me Yahweh" moment. This is how He desires to be known.

"The Lord descended in the cloud and stood with him there, and proclaimed the name of the Lord. The Lord passed before him and proclaimed, 'The Lord, the Lord, a God merciful and gracious, slow to anger, and abounding in steadfast love and faithfulness, keeping steadfast love for thousands, forgiving iniquity and transgressions and sin'" (Exodus 34:5–7a). Let's break this Scripture down, unpacking the ancient language because it's not just beautiful poetry, it's the character of our Father.

The Lord, The Lord...

When the word *Lord* is in all caps, this is Yahweh or Jehovah, the Ever-existing, Never-changing One.[15] He isn't the I was or the I will be. At whatever place we find Him, He is forever the I Am.

God

The name here means *Mighty One of Strength.*[16] He is all-powerful, yet what He chooses to do with that power is stunning.

Merciful

The Hebrew word means "to be moved with compassion or to be soft, acting in the tenderest affection."[17] Now, in our macho bravado culture, to call a dude soft is an invitation for a fight. *Don't call me soft! I'm a man!* Good thing our God is secure enough to recognize great strength in restraint. Many manly men could learn a thing or two here. His mercy doesn't draw back from brokenness but moves toward it.

Gracious

Graciousness is gentle kindness that cannot be earned.[18] It means, "to stoop in order to lift another up."[19] Jesus' invitation to cast our burdens upon His shoulders because He is gentle and humble, ready to meet our needs and grant rest to our souls, displays this aspect of God's love (Matthew 11:28–30).

Slow to Anger

At the center of God's self-description to Moses, He declares His patience. Under our translations the Hebrew means, "to delay, to defer, to wait, and to extend out over a long road before responding in anger."[20]

This is so important. We may think we see images of a rage-filled God in the Old Testament, but the preeminent credentials God uses to describe Himself are long and slow and patient. He exhausts every opportunity to meet us on our path, doing everything possible to help us experience His mercy.

The New Testament echoes in agreement that God is love, and His love is painfully patient (1 John 4:18, 1 Corinthians 13:4).

Steadfast love

This is the famous Hebrew word *chesed*, God's favorite word to describe Himself. Used 244 times in the Old Testament, it's often translated unfailing love, loyal love, or faithful love, but even these beautiful descriptions fall short. Chesed literally means, "a deep passion and burning desire to express goodness, kindness, mercy, beauty, favor, gentleness, and love to the object of one's affection, coupled with sorrow and compassion for their misfortune."[21]

Chesed expresses the Father's heart toward humanity. We may not understand some things in the story, but we can be certain our Father burns with relentless love and unrivaled tenderness. Not only that, He's abounding in it.

When I think of chesed, I think of my daughter Annabelle, who is fourteen at the time of my writing. (Fourteen going on forty.) The strongest willed of my five kids, and easily the most motivated to experience everything life has to offer, Anna is always up for an adventure. She is sweet but tough. She can cop a stronger 'tude with her mom than the best of them, but for the life of her cannot keep her room clean.

And she simply melts my heart. I am completely filled to overflowing with constant love for her. Good days and bad, she's *my girl*, and I simply can't see her through any other lens than love and delight. On the mountain, God told Moses that His love for us is like my love for my Anna.

Faithfulness

God is dependable, and we can trust His provision and support.[22] From the beginning, God has continually been the Father who will never abandon us (Deuteronomy 31:6, Hebrews 13:5).

Keeping steadfast love for thousands…

Here, chesed returns, this time with the image of God standing as a guardian. The word *keeping* celebrates God as watchman who protects us from all danger.[23] "The good shepherd lays down His life for His sheep" (John 10:11).

Forgiving iniquity and transgression and sin…

This closing triad covers the full spectrum of human failure, from the unintentional to the most sinister.

- Iniquity: "The perversity, guilt, and consequences of sin."[24]
- Transgression: "The rebellion and violation of boundaries, and the punishment for it."[25]
- Sin: "To miss the target and forfeit the prize that was supposed to be ours."[26]

And yet, despite the severity of these words, God's instinct is not to punish, but to forgive—literally, to carry the load of our sins and take them away.[27] This forgiveness isn't cheap; it's costly. But it is always His first move.

The Justice of Love

The Father concluded His introduction by warning Moses if any person demanded their power, privilege, or position to promote injustice and abuse, despite His long road of merciful patience, He would be just.

In a clever word play, Yahweh declared the Father forgives (*nasah*) all sin but cannot clear (*naqah*) it as if it never happened. He will not turn a blind eye to the injustices done to His children, allowing tormentors and abusers to wield the power of empire without consequence.

God doesn't ignore injustice. He absorbs it. He doesn't dismiss sin. He bears it. Mercy is a Person. And He looks like God revealed in Jesus.

GOD'S COMMANDMENT: WHAT HE DESIRES FOR US

The people of Israel identified 613 Laws in the Old Testament to guide their worship and way of life. Yet from the beginning, one command stood above the rest, a daily prayer that shaped their identity. It's called the *Shema*, a Hebrew word for hear. This prayer begins with a verse in Deuteronomy that says, "Hear, O Israel: The Lord our God, the Lord is one. Love the Lord your God with all your heart and with all your soul and with all your strength" (Deuteronomy 6:4–5 NIV).

Jesus later confirmed they'd done well placing this command at the center. Calling this the one law that fulfills the entire Old Testament, along with the call to love our neighbor as ourselves (Leviticus 19:18). Love has always been the goal.

We were created in love, by love, and for love. When we begin to grasp how deeply God loves us, we start to see ourselves through His eyes. In that place, love becomes more than a concept. It becomes a personal transformation. We elevate His truth over every lie of shame. We learn to extend the same grace to ourselves that He does. And out of that abundance, we begin to love others not from rigid effort, but from joyous overflow. This is the gospel. It's been the heart of God's story from the beginning.

GOD'S COMMISSION: HOW HE CHOOSES TO WORK THROUGH US

In Genesis 12, God called a man named Abram with an assignment that would shape the very mission of Israel. Pay attention to what He said to Abram.

"Go from your country and your kindred and your father's house to the land that I will show you. And I will make of you a great nation, and I will bless you...and in you all the families of the earth shall be blessed" (Genesis 12:1b, 2a, 3b).

God's intent was never for Israel to be His favorite at the world's expense but rather become a conduit of His love. Theologians estimate as many as 18,000 false gods were worshiped in the ancient Near East.[28] Amid this massive sea of deception, God called Israel to be a lighthouse, guiding lost ships back to shore. They were to be a kingdom of priests who served God, a holy nation. God chose them to be a bridge of hope to the world to demonstrate how to walk with the God of love.

This same commission echoes again in the words of Jesus.

"You are the light of the world. A city set on a hill cannot be hidden…In the same way, let your light shine before others, so that they may see your good works and give glory to your Father who is in heaven" (Matthew 5:14, 16).

Like Abram, we are called to leave every place of comfort on a mission of love that sends us to countries all over the world. Like Israel, God invites us to be a kingdom of people who serve Him, bridges of hope between heaven and earth. The mission hasn't changed. It's been misunderstood, abused, and neglected along the way, but in the heart of the Father, the mission has always remained the same.

His character is mercy.

His command is love.

His commission is to go.

This is the story we're in, and much of it, we've understood clearly. As we prepare to take a deep dive into what's really going on in the pages of the Old Testament, pause for a minute and thank God for the tapestries of grace He's woven into your sails. And as we chart onward, *hold what you've got.*

DISCUSSION QUESTIONS:

1. What aspects of God's character described in Exodus 34 (merciful, gracious, slow to anger, abounding in love and faithfulness) have you personally experienced? How do these qualities challenge or affirm your view of God when you were young?
2. Which is more difficult for you right now, receiving God's love for yourself or extending it to others? Why do you think that is?
3. God's commission to Abram was to be blessed in order to be a blessing to the world. Where have you seen the church live this out well? And where do you think we've drifted from this purpose?

FIVE

CONFLICTING KINGDOMS

How pride and violence invaded our story and why they love religion

BEFORE WE TACKLE SOME OF these practical questions. We need to recalibrate.

What about the places where God seems to be violent or angry?

What about the unspeakable deeds attributed to Him?

What about vengeance? Hell? Wrath?

Too often, we rush to defend or dismantle specific doctrines without ever stepping back to ask a deeper question. What story is the Bible trying to tell us? Remember, the Pharisees memorized the Bible and debated it masterfully, silencing their critics. And yet, they crucified the Prince of Peace as a pawn of Satan. You can persuasively argue Bible verses or theologies and completely miss the heart of God's story.

In this chapter, we will get our bearings by going back to the beginning.

- The story about Jesus.
- The story about us.
- The story about why we were created, what went wrong, and what God's been doing to bring us back to the glorious, redeeming feet of our Creator.

It's not merely a story about choosing the wrong fruit on a tree but two kingdoms in collision. Understanding from which kingdom we're living is essential.

THE KINGDOM OF LOVE AND SELF-EMPTYING SERVICE

"So God created man in his own image, in the image of God he created him; male and female he created them. And God blessed them. And God said to them, 'Be fruitful and multiply and fill the earth and subdue it, and have dominion…over every living thing that moves on the earth" (Genesis 1:27–28).

From the very beginning, our Father's desire was simple and stunning. He wanted to be with us. We were made in His image, designed to live in intimate connection with Him, just as a shadow is connected to a body. He never desired separation between us. In the perfection of Eden, God adored us and invited us to walk with Him, fully immersed in love. We were created for intimacy. We were born into a kingdom of love.

But God also created us in His likeness, with reasoning, emotion, creativity and the ability to make decisions. Like a child mirroring her parents' mannerisms, we were created to look like Him and reign with Him. As Jesus later revealed, our reign was never about domination, but self-emptying service, laying down our lives in love for one another (see Matthew 20:25–28).

And then, before God ever spoke a single command, He drew near to bless us. The Hebrew word we translate *bless* is one of my favorite glimpses into God's heart. It means, "to step from a high place down to a low one, to lift the head, to look into the eyes, to delight in, and to furnish someone with everything they will need for the journey ahead."[29]

What a picture.

Your first moment upon the earth was not one of God demanding of you. It was Him delighting in you. Blessing is the native language of His kingdom. And whether you know it yet or not, this is still true. Even now, your Father steps into the very space you occupy. He lifts your head, looks directly into your eyes as he delights to furnish absolutely everything you need. This is the kingdom of God.

In this glorious kingdom, Adam and Eve stood not merely as humans, but as son and daughter. Prince and princess. Co-rulers under the King of Creation. When God told them to *fill the earth* it wasn't just a call to multiply—it was an invitation to partner in the act of co-creating and stewarding God's fantastic creation. Joining Him to bring it to its fullest potential.[30]

This was our inheritance.

- To know the God of love, and to walk with Him as a friend
- To enjoy human love, intimacy, and partnership
- To live in joy from the overflow of His blessing
- To help the world flourish in the presence of His love

It was a kingdom of Love and Self-Emptying Service. *And it was good.*

But love must always be a choice. So, in the garden full of life, God placed a single tree with a clear warning. Do not eat of the tree of the knowledge of good and evil (Genesis 2:17). It wasn't meant to be mysterious. God plainly said this tree was poisonous. It would break us.

And that's when a serpent entered the scene.

THE KINGDOM OF PRIDE AND VIOLENCE

We're not immediately told the serpent's identity in Genesis, but Revelation later pulls back the curtain. He is the Devil (meaning slanderer or accuser).[31] His name is also Satan, the enemy.[32] If only Eve had known what Ezekiel would later pen concerning the true identity of the serpent questioning her, perhaps she would have understood the grave danger standing before her.

If only.

"You were the seal of perfection, full of wisdom and perfect in beauty. You were in Eden, the garden of God…You were anointed as a guardian cherub…You were blameless in your ways from the day you were created till wickedness was found in you. Through your widespread trade you were filled with violence, and you sinned...Your heart became proud on account of your beauty, and you corrupted your wisdom because of your splendor. So I threw you to the earth. I made you a spectacle before kings" (Ezekiel 28:12–17 NIV).

According to many scholars, this serpent was once Lucifer, an angel of light, possibly the highest-ranking of the heavenly host, entrusted with guarding heaven and leading worship. But he became prideful and his heart was filled with violence.

Pride and violence first enter the story here—twin distortions at the root of everything broken in our world. Pride, biblically, is to lift yourself up to be praised.[33] It's to center the world around yourself. It's the idolatry of self over others, creation, and even God. Violence, from the Hebrew *hāmās*, means, "to cause harm or injustice, to exploit, to violate, to display cruelty physically, emotionally, spiritually, or ethically."[34]

Violence can take two forms.

- **Active violence**—using one's power to hurt, oppress, or slander. Physical, emotional, or spiritual abuse.
- **Passive violence**—withholding love, justice, presence, or protection when it's in one's power to give it. Physical, emotional, or spiritual neglect.

Active violence is a sin of commission (I hurt you). Passive violence is a sin of omission (I ignored your pain). Both are violent. Both dehumanize the image of God in others and oppose the way of love.

As Jesus would later show us about the nature of all sin, violence is not chiefly defined by an action, but rather an attitude in the heart that results in harmful action or inaction. It is the attitude of pride in the heart that makes an action violent. As opposed to an action that protects justice or peace on behalf of a loved one. This distinction cannot be overstated.

From the moment the term violence (hāmās) erupted on the scene through Lucifer, this word went on to be used sixty times in the Bible. Fallen humanity and even the system of the world filled with violence is attributed to him. But violence is never attributed to God.[35]

The Old Testament points to frequent prayers from the children of God to be rescued from violence.[36] Isaiah promised the coming Messiah would not walk in violence or deceit (Isaiah 53:9). Instead, He would come as the One who saves us *from* violence.[37] Isaiah again proclaimed that the evidence of God's kingdom coming to earth would be that violence's reign would end (Isaiah 60:18). Violence is not God's nature. It had no place in creation before Lucifer's fall, and it will have no home in the future that awaits us. Violence is nothing more than the fruit of pride, the badge of a counterfeit kingdom.

Come back to the Garden of Eden with me. Lucifer was stripped of his heavenly office, cast to the earth "as a spectacle before kings" (Ezekiel 28:17). Do you remember our created position in Eden? We were royalty. Lucifer and the third of heaven under his authority fell to the earth, stripped of the pomp that made them proud, yet not destroyed (Revelation 12:4).

Mercy allowed them to live.

The king of pride and violence had no kingdom. The kings and queens of the earth, the beloved children of God, had only one charge to obey. We were to keep ourselves uncorrupted by the pursuit of wisdom. But if anyone knew how to play on ego, it was Lucifer, who shifted from being a protector of humanity to an agent set on destroying it. Later, Satan would be seen as the one who in every way represented the *opposite* of the purposes of God.

- Jesus appears as the Christ (Matthew 16:16). So, Satan makes an appearance as anti-Christ (1 John 4:3).
- Jesus comes as the light of the world (John 8:12). Satan arrives as the prince of darkness (Ephesians 6:12).
- Jesus is the truth (John 14:6). Satan is the father of lies (John 8:44).
- Jesus is the advocate (1 John 2:1). Satan is the accuser (Revelation 12:10).
- Jesus is the God of heaven (Genesis 24:3). So, Satan plots to become the god of this age (2 Corinthians 4:4).

Two kings reign in our story. One is the true King, the Father, expressed completely in Jesus of Nazareth. The other a false king, a tyrant but powerful nonetheless. After all, he coerced the sons and daughters of God to abdicate their favored position for the chains of slavery.

Worst of all, to this day, many of the greatest promoters of his regime don't even realize whose agenda they serve, because he is disguised as an angel of light. The closets of the spirit of pride are filled with religious garments and moralistic shoes worn to assault those loved by God...*in the name of God.*

Lord, help us.

The serpent appealed to humanity's pride, calling us to think about ourselves, provide for ourselves, and to taste and see for ourselves. Eve looked at the fruit and saw it didn't appear poisonous. It was pleasing to her eye, making her stomach rumble with desire. And somehow, it promised wisdom. It offered control. She would be the master of her own destiny.

Understand, ignorance didn't lead Eve to take the fruit. Arrogance did. Paul would later write, Eve "was deceived" (1 Timothy 2:14). It is helpful to note that the word translated as *deceived* also means seduced.[38] Her deception was no innocent mistake, like accidentally forgetting to scan an item in the checkout line. It is far more like someone deciding to rob a bank while failing to understand that the vault they risked everything for was empty. Oh, and before anyone recites the tired "Let's blame Eve for humanity's problems" banter, let me remind all of us that Adam stood by silently, offering no resistance, no covering, no courage. Humanity fell. You fell. And I fell.

We were made for intimacy, and we chose independence. This was the sin in the garden. We crowned self.

Self-preservation.

Self-help.

Self-fulfillment.

Self-rule.

In so doing, we handed over the keys of the kingdom to a fallen tyrant.

The consequences came swiftly. Their eyes were opened, but instead of godlike wisdom, they gained shame. They covered themselves. They hid from God. And when God called to them, pride led to violence again.

God turned to Adam. And Adam, knowing the penalty for eating the fruit was death, didn't hesitate to place the blame on Eve, whom he refused to even address by name, calling her simply, "This woman you gave me…" (Genesis 3:12 paraphrase). In turn, Eve placed the blame on the serpent. Everyone ducked responsibility, reducing the dignity of co-rule to accusation and self-preservation.

The pride of living for myself always leads to violence toward you.

Always.

But then something remarkable happened.

God didn't come running in with destruction. He came walking. *He came low.* He asked questions. And even as He acknowledged the real consequences of sin—relational breakdown, painful labor, hierarchy, and death—He declared something Satan didn't expect.

Hope.

God declared the serpent's deception an act of war. For a time, Satan would be:

- The spirit that is now at work in the sons of disobedience. (Ephesians 2:2)
- The ruler of this world. (John 14:30)
- The god of this age. (2 Corinthians 4:4 NIV)
- The authority over the dark world and the spiritual forces in heavenly realms. (Eph. 6:12 NIV)
- The deceiver of the whole world. (Revelation 12:9)

But from the very first moment of our fall, God informed the enemy of our souls that this story was not going to go as he hoped. Far from abandoning humanity to our deserved end, our Father drew us close and promised the end of Satan's kingdom through a divine-human deliverer.

"I will put enmity between you and the woman, and between your offspring and her offspring; he shall bruise your head, and you shall bruise his heel" (Genesis 3:15).

The very womb that faced shame would one day bring forth a Deliverer. Death would not have the final word. The King would return.

The war had begun. It wasn't a war over a tree or rules to follow, but a battle for the very heart of humanity. It still is. Two kings and two kingdoms exist, and we will give ourselves entirely to one or the other. We must choose.

- The kingdom of self-emptying love. Loving God with all my heart always leads me to empty myself in love for others.
- The kingdom of pride and violence. Living for myself always ends up harming others.

In the days following the rebellion in Eden, God ushered Adam and Eve out of the Garden—not in vengeance, but in mercy. It was His first act of rescue, removing us from the Garden, so we wouldn't eat from the Tree of Life and remain forever in our fallen condition. He left two angels to guard the entrance, removing us from the Garden of God but not from the Presence of God. From that very moment, God walked *with* us in the wilderness of our own choosing, guiding our hearts toward the day of His coming promise.

But pride and violence ran deep. Within one generation, we shed blood in the pursuit of blessing. Within a few more, we built entire systems of religion to justify harming others in God's name all in hopes of securing a love He'd already freely given.

Yet God never fights darkness with darkness. He doesn't wield the tools of Satan to cast out Satan. Instead, our Father chooses *to go low*—meeting us in the dust, offering mercy, slowing our collapse. He gave us laws and leaders, prophets and promises not to coerce us, but to reveal His heart and slow our ruin until the fullness of time came.

That's the topic of our next chapter.

DISCUSSION QUESTIONS

1. In what ways do you see the kingdom of pride and violence influencing the world around you or even creeping into your own thinking? Where do you notice the temptation to live for ourselves, and how might that impact others?
2. The chapter highlights that God responded to humanity's rebellion not merely with punishment, but with protection and a promise. How does this truth reshape your view of God's character and His response to our failures?
3. We often justify harmful actions, even religious ones, in the name of preserving blessing or truth. Where have you seen religion used to promote pride or violence? How can we be people who embody the kingdom of self-emptying love instead?

SIX

FOGGY POTS AND FUNHOUSE MIRRORS

How we've misread God in the pages

"FOR NOW WE SEE IN A MIRROR DIMLY, but then face to face. Now I know in part; then I shall know fully, even as I have been fully known" (1 Corinthians 13:12).

In Paul's day, mirrors were nothing like the ones we use to shave or apply mascara. They were polished metal—blurry, warped, and barely reflective. Think of trying to see your reflection in the bottom of a cooking pot. You might make out basic shapes and colors, but everything else would be distorted, like a funhouse mirror at a carnival.

Paul uses this image to describe how we see God, not with perfect clarity, but through riddles and enigmas.[39] We only know in part, but what we do know can be trusted with all our hearts. That said, much still remains a mystery.

But he did offer us two words of encouragement. First, this mirror is not permanent. One day we'll see God face to face. And second, even in our partial vision, God sees us clearly. While we wait to fully know, we are fully known.

If Paul, arguably the clearest theological mind in history, could admit he didn't fully grasp the mysteries of God, perhaps we can relax our grip too. Much of our frustration comes when we treat the Bible like a Magic 8 Ball. We ask a question and then shake our Bibles, open to a verse searching for an answer to tell us who to marry, whether or not to take the promotion, or which political candidate might be the Antichrist. The Bible doesn't work that way. Remember, Scripture is inspired. Our interpretation is not. Let's take it one step further. The Bible is inspired for the purposes God intended.

Our Bible has been passed down through prophets, scribes, and translators over many generations, because God is telling a story. It's not a relationship manual or a self-help book. It's the story of His heart, and God chose a method for telling it. We've never encountered another book like it. We need to handle this one with care.

I've spent years studying how the Bible came to be. I've dug into its original languages and committed countless hours in background study, commentaries, and context. I found a lot our Father chose to do that I never would've had the guts to do if it were my story. He took major risks entrusting His biography to shady characters who would have trouble passing a background check today. He stood resolute as humanity reached shocking new lows in history, continuing to move slowly to unveil His true nature.

He's allowed us to accuse, assault, and armchair quarterback His character for centuries, to the present day. We have believed and taught some terrible things about God, and yet He has stayed the course. He's done it all to progressively reveal the goodness of His heart, to any willing to listen, absorbing the abuse of critics and naysayers, and loving them still.

In this chapter, we'll survey the Old Testament in twelve key movements where God came low to reform our understanding of His heart. In each place, He urged us to leave the kingdom of pride and violence and to surrender to our need for a Savior. But it seems we were convinced, given enough time and resources, we could somehow right the ship ourselves. These twelve reform plans are not unexpected detours, but God's very goodness to preserve our lives and to carry us forward to the day of His coming.

As we read, we'll see vengeance does not drive the theme of the Old Testament. We were already dead in our sins. This story is about rescue.

In the next chapter, we'll explore the world in which these stories were written and uncover truths the original audience understood intuitively, many of which we've missed. But for now, let's begin with what God was doing through it all.

FAILED ATTEMPTS AT REFORM AWAITING FIERCE RESCUE

"When we were children, we were enslaved to the elementary principles of the world. But when the fullness of time had come, God sent forth his Son, born of woman, born under the law, to redeem those who were under the law, so that we might receive adoption as sons. And because you are sons, God has sent the Spirit of his Son into our hearts, crying, 'Abba! Father!'" (Galatians 4:3b–6).

For years, I wrestled with the phrase the *fullness of time*. If humanity needed a Savior from the beginning, why didn't Jesus come sooner? Why wasn't the cross planted right outside the Garden? Wouldn't that have saved us years of bloodshed and heartbreak? But these questions miss something essential. The fullness of time wasn't about God needing more time. It was for us.

God has always been ready. Christ died for us even when we fought against Him (Romans 5:10). More than that, the Lamb was already slain before God separated the light from darkness and formed the world, outside of time and space (Revelation 13:8). He only needed to be revealed during these last days for our sake (1 Peter 1:20). We were the ones who needed to come to the end of our own strength. The fullness of time arrived when all our attempts at self-salvation failed.

God is and has always been the God of love and self-emptying service. He doesn't force. He refuses to manipulate. Instead, He waits, He invites, and He woos.

In the Garden, self-emptying love gave us the dignity of choice. This love didn't retaliate but promised redemption. Self-emptying love led us out of the Garden, going with us, never once abandoning His children.

From the very beginning, God chose to be with us, revealing His heart, inviting us to trust Him, and moving patiently down a long road of mercy to save us from ourselves. This is not the story of a wrathful God slowly warming to love, but of a loving God who bore every wrath upon Himself, so we could be together again.

The pain we encounter through the Old Testament is largely self-inflicted, and we would do well to remember, technically speaking, the Law was never supposed to work. We cannot become righteous by following the Law. Thus, the reform plans God gives His children in the Old Testament are designed simply to convince us of our need for a Savior.

"Why then was the law given at all? It was given alongside the promise to show people their sins. But the law was designed to last only until the coming of the 'Seed,' the child who was promised" (Galatians 3:19 TPT).

God's promise in the Garden preceded the Law. God would come back for His children and He would establish them. In this sense, the Old Testament chronicles failed attempts at reform, to help us see clearly that no amount of human strategy or ingenuity could fix our sin problem. We needed new hearts.

Sadly, we were, and often still are, slow to learn. At every major reform plan God offered for our healing, we seemed to fall into the same tragic traps. Praise God, our Father was never content to leave us there.

THE PATTERN OF THE OLD TESTAMENT

As we read the story, a seven-fold pattern begins to emerge.

1. God calls humanity to walk in intimacy with Him, and from that union, to release love, mercy, and hope over creation.
2. We choose pride.
3. Our pride leads to violence.
4. Our pride and violence have real consequences and release death on the earth.
5. God continually goes low in love to serve humanity and rescue as many as will follow Him, to lead humanity to His promised deliverer, Jesus.
6. In mercy, God permits or provides humanity a reform as a speed bump to delay our freely chosen destruction of ourselves

and one another.

7. In pride, we trust the reform to save us. We continually fail, and God again points humanity to His initial promise and invitation to intimacy.

We see this pattern start immediately, a stone's throw from Eden.

A PREVIEW OF THE OLD TESTAMENT:

'Failed Reforms Awaiting Fierce Rescue'

CAIN & ABEL:	The Next Generation Can't Save Us (GEN. 4-5)
NOAH:	'Starting Over' Can't Save Us (GEN. 6:1-8:19)
SACRIFICES:	Religious Activities Can't Save Us (GEN. 8:20-11:32)
ABRAHAM:	A Nation Can't Save Us (GEN. 12-50)
MOSES:	An Influential Leader Can't Save Us (EX. 1-18)
LAWS:	A 'Godly Government' Can't Save Us (EX. 19-DEUT. 34)
PROMISED LAND:	New Surroundings/Circumstances Can't Save Us (JOSH. 1-24)
JUDGES:	Leaders Can't Save Us (JUDGES 1-21)
RUTH:	(Selah) A Preview of the One who Can Save Us (RUTH 1-4)
KINGS:	Kings Can't Save Us (1 SAM. 1-2 CHRON. 36)
PROPHETS:	Preachers Can't Save Us (1 KGS, ESTHER-EZRA, IS.-MAL.)
JOB:	Avoiding Suffering Can't Save Us (JOB 1-42)
ECCLESIASTES:	Pursuing Pleasure Can't Save Us (ECCL. 1-12)
KINGDOM SONGS:	(Selah) A Preview of the One who Can Save Us (PSALMS, PROVERBS, SONG OF SOLOMON)

CAIN AND ABEL: THE NEXT GENERATION CAN'T SAVE US (GENESIS 4–5)

Outside the Garden, Eve became pregnant. God set His first reform plan in motion. Humanity would continue. A child was born who was not directly involved in Eden's rebellion. Hope rose. Eve named her son Cain. His name meant "spear of my possession; my weapon."[40] Eve proclaimed, "With the help of the Lord, I have brought forth a man" (Genesis 4:1 NIV).

In the naming of her son, we hear not only gratitude but signs of trouble. Many scholars believe Eve viewed Cain as the promised seed—her weapon, who would crush the serpent and return the kingdom she'd lost.

Old Testament scholar Bruce Waltke alluded to it. "Although acknowledging the Lord's role in procreation here, the naming betrays a synergism. Essentially Eve said, 'I have done this.' The reader is signaled to expect problems in the life and line of Cain."[41]

That signal arrived quickly. Cain grew up alongside his younger brother, Abel. In time, both bring offerings to the Lord. Abel gave the first and best of his flock, while Cain brought some of his crops. God honored Abel's whole-hearted gift but not Cain's half-hearted one. Cain became furious with God and burned with jealousy against his brother.

But God didn't scold him. Instead, He came low, just as He had with Adam and Eve. He warned Cain of sin's desire to master him and invites him into intimacy, "If you do what is right, will you not be accepted?" (Genesis 4:7 NIV). But Cain would have no part of it. In the field, jealousy boils over, and Cain murders his brother.

Here, humanity's sin escalated. Adam and Eve hid in shame. Cain stood in the open. They tried to blame one another but didn't deny their sin. Cain sarcastically and brazenly lied to God's face.

But note God's response to Cain's sin. He didn't punish or retaliate. Instead, He marked Cain—not for judgment, but for *protection*, so no one would do to Cain as he did to his brother. Our God answered murder with mercy. However, in just a few generations, Cain's descendant Lamech distorted God's kindness as a license for unbridled vengeance as he used Cain's mark to kill without consequence, in God's name (Genesis 4:23–24).

The next generation couldn't save us.

NOAH: STARTING OVER CAN'T SAVE US (GENESIS 6:1–8:19)

"The Lord saw that the wickedness of man was great in the earth, and that every intention of the thoughts of his heart was only evil continually. And the Lord regretted that he had made man on the earth, and it grieved him to his heart" (Genesis 6:5–6 NIV).

As humanity multiplied, so did our appetite for violence. When the text says, "The wickedness of man was great," it literally means they had become very bad. Consider the irony. The very creation that was once very good became its own opposite. Even more sobering, the word *wick-*

ed also means malignant and highly contagious.[42] Humanity's violence, both passive and active, had infected the earth like a terminal disease.

"Now the earth was corrupt [*šāḥaṯ*] in God's sight, and the earth was filled with violence. And God saw the earth, and behold, it was corrupt [šāḥaṯ], for all flesh had corrupted [šāḥaṯ] their way on the earth. And God said to Noah, 'I have determined to make an end [šāḥaṯ] of all flesh, for the earth is filled with violence through them" (Genesis 6:11–13 NIV).

The Hebrew word *šāḥaṯ* appears four times in this short passage and is translated as both corrupt and destroy. It's a word of self-destruction. The earth was not simply being judged. It was unraveling under its own sin.

But what is God's response in Genesis 6:5–6? Read it again.

Not rage.

Not vengeance.

Heartbreak.

The two Hebrew verbs in Genesis 6:6 (regretted and grieved) describe profound emotional pain. The first means to mourn and experience deep suffering.[43] The other means to be stabbed or pierced and broken into pieces.[44] The author of Genesis painted an image of a Father whose heart has been torn open. God was not an angry tyrant lashing out in frustration. He's a grieving parent, devastated by what His children became and the chaos they unleashed. As Greg Boyd observed, "When God saw that his merciful striving had no hope of turning the earth's landlords around, he had no choice but to withdraw his Spirit, thereby allowing sāhat [corruption] to reap its own sāhat [destruction]."[45]

Though He had every right, God was not portrayed as an angry executioner, eager to destroy humanity. Humanity had already destroyed itself, even as the earth under their care followed its lead. The virus of sin had infected everything, even the ground entrusted to human care.

Everything.

Everything except Noah.

The narrative now shifts from heartbroken Father to Rescuer. God seeks out the one man still willing to listen and promises to rescue his family by placing them in an ark. This word appears only one other time in Scripture where it describes the basket that hid Moses from the slaughter of Hebrew babies. The ark was not an instrument of judgment. It was a vessel of rescue in the midst of judgment.

The scene of the flood does involve judgment. To argue anything else would be trying to superimpose a secret meaning over the text, while turning a blind eye to arguably the most catastrophic event of recorded history. There was judgment and it was tied directly to mankind's idolatrous desire to live as gods, releasing great violence upon the earth. But God was not found seated far away in the recesses of heaven as a calloused and indifferent judge. Neither was He raging on the scene as an angry executioner. He was the one running into the eye of the hurricane rescuing anyone who would follow Him out of the hellscape we created.

When the waters finally receded, God sealed a promise with a sign in the sky. A rainbow. Growing up, this always felt like an odd, even unrelated, provision. The earth had been decimated, but here was a rainbow?

It may help to understand that the word translated *rainbow* is the word for a "war bow," the curved weapon used for battle. The imagery would not have been lost to ancient readers.

Look closely at the picture.

First, God's weapon was pure light, refracted into radiant, beaming color. The God, who is light, does not employ the weapons of darkness.

Second, notice where the bow was aimed. Not toward the earth. The bow was turned upward, at the heavens. This was no sentimental decoration. It was a declaration. Scripture repeatedly describes Satan as ruling the broken systems of the world as "the prince of the power of the air" (Ephesians 2:2). Paul also called him and the fallen angels cosmic powers over darkness, and evil spiritual forces of the heavens (Ephesians 6:12).

The rainbow, much like the mark placed upon Cain, was a gift of protection. For humanity, it flipped on the lights, exposing the ruin of violence and calling us out from the shadows to live as lights in the world. To the powers of darkness, it stretched across the heavens like a warning shot that God protects and will ultimately redeem the world He loves.

Once Noah's feet touched dry land, God established a covenant with him, just as He made with Adam. But the story ends with a familiar tragedy. Noah, the only righteous man on earth, planted a vineyard, drank himself into a stupor, and then passed out, uncovering his nakedness for his sons to see (Genesis 9:21–22).

We had been given a fresh start. But the human heart hadn't changed. Starting over wasn't going to save us.

SACRIFICES: RELIGIOUS ACTIVITY CAN'T SAVE US (GENESIS 8:20–11:32)

After the flood, Noah built an altar to the Lord and offered sacrifices, a gesture of renewed commitment to trust and follow God's ways—*to fill all the earth and subdue it* as originally commanded. Yet, only chapters later, humanity united for a very different purpose. They wanted to build a tower to heaven.

"'Come, let us make bricks, and burn them thoroughly.'... Then they said, 'Come, let us build ourselves a city and a tower with its top in the heavens, and let us make a name for ourselves, lest we be dispersed over the face of the whole earth'" (Genesis 11:3–4).

The irony is breathtaking. In Genesis 1, God looked upon the dust and said, "Let us make a man." This man would bear God's own image and name (Genesis 1:26). Here, humanity looked upon that same dust, burned it into bricks, and said, "Let us make a tower," through which they could elevate their own name. God breathed in the dust to release life that would fill the earth. Man seized the dust to constrain and control it, to make a monument of pride to himself.

They built a ziggurat, a tower with a room at the top where they believed the gods would come to serve their desires. God's reply was humorous. They imagined an impressive estate that would demand the attention of the gods, but the Scripture says God had to *come down*. In Hebrew, this word means to "lay prostrate."[46] The implied picture imagines the Creator of galaxies with His face pressed to the ground, trying to detect the tiny structure humanity considered their highest achievement. Even still, the response is striking. God came down.

He doesn't respond in anger or violence. He merely gave another speed bump of mercy to slow our self-destruction by confusing our languages, so we would disperse and fill the earth He made for our blessing and habitation. The confusion of language wasn't merely a judgment. It was preservation. A gracious blessing from the God who again decided to empty Himself to serve us and steer us back to our original call.

Still, the cost of our pride was steep. Tribalism, nationalism, and war began to define the generations. But how beautiful that, when the Spirit fell at Pentecost, God reversed Babel. All the nations of the world heard Him again as one (Acts 2:8). That said, the disaster in Babel showed firsthand the destructive power people can wield in the name of religion.

Sacrifices cannot save us.

ABRAHAM: A NATION CAN'T SAVE US (GENESIS 12–50)

As nations began to form across the earth, God set out to create a lighthouse—something visible and tangible through which humanity could once again recognize His goodness amidst a sea of counterfeit gods. So, He chose a man named Abram and made a promise.

"Go from your country and your kindred and your father's house to the land that I will show you. And I will make of you a great nation, and I will bless you and make your name great, so that you will be a blessing… and in you all the families of the earth shall be blessed" (Genesis 12:1–3).

This promise, known as the Abrahamic covenant, was not about favoritism but mission. God longed to form a people who would trust Him so fully, and reflect Him so clearly, that through them all the families of the earth could come to know the One True God. The Father does not change, and His love has always reached His global children made in His image.

In faith, Abram set out with his wife Sarai to the land God had promised. But soon after Abram arrived, fear led to compromise with the most precious thing God had given him. His bride. Fearing Pharaoh might kill him to take his wife, Abram told Sarai to lie and say she was his sister. Sarai was taken into Pharaoh's house, exploited, and only released after plagues revealed God's protective hand. The damage, however, was already done to Sarai's dignity, to Pharaoh's household, and to the witness of Abram's God. So much for being a blessing to the nations.

Years passed. Sarai remained barren. Though God had promised them a son, they decided to help Him out. Following the custom of the surrounding cultures, Abram slept with Sarai's servant, Hagar, to produce an heir. The fallout was heartbreaking. Hagar was mistreated, and the child born from that union, Ishmael, became the root of generations of conflict. And yet—what did God do? *He came low.* He saw Hagar in her exile and called her by name. He rescued her. He blessed her son. And He returned again to Abram and Sarai with mercy, giving another opportunity to obey Him. A year later, Isaac was born, the son of promise.

But even with God's personal intervention and the establishment of the Israelite people, it was clear.

A nation cannot save us.

MOSES: AN INFLUENTIAL LEADER CAN'T SAVE US (EXODUS 1–18)

Fast forward. The descendants of Abraham multiplied into a mighty people, but a new Pharaoh arose in Egypt—one who didn't know Israel's God. Fearful of their growing strength, he enslaved them, ordering the systematic murder of every Hebrew baby boy.

And what did God do?

He came low.

God provided an ark—a vessel of rescue—for a Hebrew baby named Moses. Miraculously, Moses was raised in Pharaoh's palace as a son of Egypt. Yet Moses came to know his true identity and longed to see his people set free. But like so many before him, pride and violence came easily. One day, seeing an Egyptian beating a Hebrew, Moses lashed out and killed the man, burying his body in the sand (Exodus 2:12). When the truth came out, Moses fled into the desert.

And what did God do?

He came low.

In the wilderness, God patiently refined the fiery prince into a humble shepherd before revealing Himself through fire itself. Through a bush that blazed but was not consumed, God called Moses back into intimacy and into mission.

Through signs and wonders, God sent Moses to confront Pharaoh. His goal wasn't just to free the Israelites; it was also to woo the Egyptians, to show them their gods were powerless, and He alone was good, just, and worthy of worship.

Each plague directly confronted a prominent Egyptian deity.

The Egyptian god Osiris boasted the Nile was his bloodstream, so the river was turned to blood to demonstrate his powerlessness next to the God of Israel. What's more, the Egyptians drowned thousands of Hebrew babies in these very waters. At that moment, they were confronted with the death they had unleashed within their streams.[47]

Their goddess Heqet was believed to be the goddess of birth who had the head of a frog. Because of this, frogs were sacred to the Egyptians and stepping on one could be punished by death. In the second plague, through a dual irony, the land was filled with frogs being born at an uncontrolled rate, and stepping on one was inevitable because so many covered the land. It was a patient plea to come to their senses.

Each sign was a merciful confrontation, an invitation to Pharaoh to release the people and renounce the kingdom of pride and violence. But he refused. He continued to harden his heart, doubling down on slavery, brutality, and the slaughter of innocents. Finally, judgment came, and his reign of terror ran out. Like the men of Genesis 6, Pharaoh chose total destruction. The details of the end of Egypt's plagues break my heart, on a grand scale. But even here, the Father was at work as the Rescuer of a brutally enslaved people. He patiently pleaded for the spiritual slavery of Egypt to be broken as well, but they were not willing. So, at great cost, Israel was freed.

But soon after the Israelites walked through a split Red Sea onto dry land, the people began to grumble against Moses and against God. Some even longed to return to slavery. Moses was regarded as the most patient man on earth (Numbers 12:3). He endured decades of complaining. But even he cracked.

One day, desperate for water, the people turned on Moses. God instructed Moses to speak to a rock, and water would flow, showing that He, their Rock, was faithful to provide. But Moses, tired of not being respected by the people, roared at them as he struck the rock not once, but twice, "Must we bring you water out of this rock?" (Numbers 20:10–11 NIV).

Water came, but the moment marked the end of Moses' leadership. He would not enter the Promised Land. Why? Because the kingdom of pride and violence is completely at odds with the kingdom of God.

And yet, how did God respond?

He didn't strike Moses, as Moses had struck the rock. He didn't shame him. *He came low.*

God brought Moses to a high mountain, allowed him to gaze at the Promised Land, and met with him there. And in gentleness, He brought home His beloved friend in peace.

A leader, even the most patient one who ever lived, couldn't save us.

LAWS: A GODLY GOVERNMENT CAN'T SAVE US (EXODUS 19–DEUTERONOMY 34)

After leading Israel out of Egypt, God brought Moses to Mt. Sinai to receive a new reform plan, a set of laws designed to govern the people. These weren't given to save Israel or earn them favor with God, but to guide, protect, and set boundaries for wandering people with wayward hearts. The New Testament later makes this clear.

The law is only a shadow of the good things that are coming—not the realities themselves…it can never make perfect those who draw near (Hebrews 10:1 NIV).

What the law was powerless to do…God did by sending his own Son (Romans 8:3 NIV).

The Law was not a permanent solution. It was a gracious speed bump—a temporary system to slow down our self-destruction until the fullness of time came. It was never a complete revelation of God's heart but a shadow in which He met His people and pointed to something greater.

Over time, Jewish worshipers categorized the 613 commandments into civil, ceremonial, and moral laws. These laws reflected the specific temptations and cultural challenges of their day. They were to help Israel live distinctly among the surrounding nations, called, not to blend in, but to stand out as a people devoted to Yahweh.

Some laws, like the Ten Commandments, expressed timeless moral truths affirmed by Jesus and echoed through the New Testament. Others, like dietary restrictions or purity codes, were cultural and designed to train the people in holiness marking them as belonging to God.

Take, for example, their command to build a fence on the roof of their homes (Deuteronomy 22:8). God's not a moody homeowner's association president. Ancient homes had flat roofs where families hosted gatherings. With no electric lighting, guests could fall to serious injury or even death if someone failed to line their roof with a fence. This law was a practical application to protect those in our care, much like our seatbelt laws.

But when we apply Old Testament laws without context or cultural understanding, we distort the image of God. We make Him seem petty or punitive, reducing the gospel to a code of behavior. Even Israel couldn't keep them fully. And that, in part, was the point.

Go with me back to Sinai where Moses spent forty days in the presence of God receiving the Law. He came down the mountain radiating with excitement to call his countrymen into the freedom of obedience...until he saw the unthinkable. The people were throwing a rager. Music, food, dancing, and shouting filled the camp, but the God of Israel wasn't the honored guest.

They bowed before a golden calf they fashioned out of the spoils of Egypt, worshiping the inanimate statue as the god who led them to freedom. Now, I don't know how much wine you've got to drink before you confuse the God who parts the sea with a cow figurine, but they had one or two drinks beyond that! Infuriated, Moses called the people to account. Before he could even deliver the Law, they'd already abandoned it.

Laws would not save us.

PROMISED LAND: NEW SURROUNDINGS AND CIRCUMSTANCES CAN'T SAVE US (JOSHUA 1–24)

When Moses' life ended, leadership passed to his protégé, Joshua.

Talk about impossible shoes to fill. Yet God assured Joshua of His continued presence. He told him three times to be "strong and courageous" (Joshua 1:6, 7, 9). Joshua would lead the people across the Jordan into the land He promised Abraham.

At the water's edge, God again met His people. As the priests carrying the Ark of the Covenant stepped into the river, the Jordan receded, mirroring the Red Sea crossing, as dry ground stretched out before them, just as it was with Moses.

Their first test in the land was Jericho, a fortress city locked down and impenetrable. Here, God gave bizarre instructions to march around the city for seven days with trumpets, pots, and pans like a middle school marching band. No weapons. Just worship. On the seventh day, the walls collapsed. Without lifting a sword, God brought the victory.

Then came the battle of Ai. Riding the high of victory and convinced they were unstoppable, Israel rushed in—and were routed. It was a humiliating defeat. Joshua cried out to God, confused and heartbroken.

And *God came low.*

He confided in Joshua that someone in their camp had clung to idols. This wasn't about stealing some trinkets. The statues hidden in the tent, left unchecked, would soon be false saviors in the tabernacles of their hearts.

This painfully foreshadowed a people who would spend the coming generations trying to stand with one foot in two conflicting kingdoms. They wanted the blessings of God while harboring the gods of pride and violence in the inner recesses of their hearts.

The reform under Joshua would fall short, as Israel failed to fully occupy the land of promise. A new zip code doesn't change an old heart.

New surroundings couldn't save us.

JUDGES: LEADERS CAN'T SAVE US (JUDGES 1–21)

"In those days there was no king in Israel. Everyone did what was right in his own eyes" (Judges 17:6).

By the time we reach the book of Judges, Israel is unraveling. After the death of Joshua, they find themselves in a free fall of rebellion and defeat.

And *God came low.*

He raised up judges who would rescue the people from their war and waywardness and bring them back into peace. Yet, despite God's continual nearness—His mercy, His revelation, His guidance—they still believed that with enough time, strength, and human effort, they could save themselves. They were addicted to what was right in their own eyes.

The result is a grim, repetitive spiral, which continued throughout the book of Judges.

1. Israel turned from God in pride and embraced violence.
2. Their choices carried consequences and they experienced defeat.
3. Eventually, they cried out to God.
4. God, in mercy, raised up a judge to rescue and lead them.
5. Peace lasted as long as the judge lived.
6. The judge died, and the people returned to pride and rebellion.
7. Rinse and repeat.

The author of Judges deliberately structured this book to show a downward trajectory. Each cycle didn't merely repeat. It worsened. Understand, this wasn't a judgment from God but evidence of His mercy. Each judge acted as a gracious speed bump to provide some semblance of order, helping to slow the people's self-destruction.

Early on, we meet one of Scripture's brightest lights, a woman leading in a patriarchal world where women had little voice.

Deborah's most significant acts of bravery came when Israel's military commander, Barak, lacked the courage to lead his troops. Armed with nothing but faith, Deborah led the people to victory. And when it was over, she gave all honor to the God of heaven.

By the end of the book, we meet Samson, Israel's final judge—a tragic foil to Deborah. In places where she had no voice but led with wisdom, Samson drowned in privilege yet squandered it all for pleasure.

Samson was a Nazirite, a man set apart by several vows. His commitments included the following:

- No wine.
- No touching dead things.

- No intermarrying among idol-worshiping nations (Judges 13:4, Numbers 6:3).

And as quickly as possible, he shattered every semblance of obedience to God. He demanded a Philistine bride. He threw a drunken wedding party. And he ate honey from a rotting lion's corpse that he shared with his parents, defiling them without their knowledge (Judges 14). Samson was brash, reckless, and egotistical. Not once does Samson act on behalf of Israel. His only concern was his self-gratification.

Eventually, he fell in love with Delilah, a prostitute enlisted by the Philistines to uncover his secret. When she seduced him and shaved his head in his sleep (violating one of his Nazirite vows), Samson's strength departed. But he didn't realize the presence of God was gone.

That's a prophetic statement in more ways than one. All these years, Samson had built his own empire based on possessions, pleasure, and power, and he assumed God was on his side. He'd baptized his own kingdom in religious imagery and never stopped to see God was nothing like all the things Samson did in His name.

The Philistines gouged out Samson's eyes and made him their entertainment. And what did God do?

He came low.

God allowed Samson's hair to grow again. In the silence of captivity, the once-mighty judge had time to retrace his downfall to the root of his pride. Stripped of sight, strength, and status, perhaps now Samson could see more clearly than ever before. This was mercy—God whispering that even now, Samson had a chance to be who he was created to be. But Samson would have none of it.

Samson only prayed twice in his lifetime. Once, to demand God give him something to drink like an agitated diner at a restaurant (Judges 15:18). And here. He did not pray for forgiveness or wisdom. Not even for Israel. He prayed for vengeance against the Philistines for taking his eyes. And in his final act, Samson collapsed the pillars, killing himself and his enemies in a blaze of violence.

The book closes with Israel at an all-time low. Rather than being set apart, they had become just like the ungodly nations surrounding them. They no longer looked like the people of God. They looked like Samson. It was unmistakably clear.

Leaders cannot save us.

RUTH (SELAH): A PREVIEW OF THE ONE WHO CAN SAVE US (RUTH 1–4)

After the long shadows cast by Judges, the book of Ruth offers a tender, hope-filled interlude—a deep breath of grace in a dark hour. It's the story of a foreign woman who lost everything yet remained faithful. She sold herself into service just to survive but found redemption through an unexpected act of love.

Boaz, a kinsman-redeemer, a noble man with the legal right to marry her and restore her inheritance, bought Ruth back. He didn't just meet the minimum requirements of the law; he exceeded them, showering Ruth with kindness, dignity, and protection.

In a time of violence and chaos, the story of Ruth was one of compassion and covenant. And it ends with a promise. Boaz became the great-grandfather of King David, from whose line the Messiah, our true Redeemer, would one day come.

Ruth is more than a love story. It's a preview. A glimpse of the One who would come to redeem the world—not by obligation, but by choice. Jesus is our Kinsman-Redeemer. *He alone can save us.* And the One who delights to do so.

KINGS: KINGS CAN'T SAVE US (1 SAMUEL 1–2, CHRONICLES 36)

The story picks back up with humanity still clinging to the kingdom of pride, still convinced salvation can be seized through power, control, or charisma. And as always, the pride of living for me inevitably leads to violence toward you.

Although God called Israel to be set apart, they longed to blend in, so they demanded for the prophet Samuel to give them a king (1 Samuel 8:5). This devastated Samuel. He knew they weren't just asking for a leader. They were rejecting the kingship of God Himself. But what did God do?

He came low.

With heartbreaking grace, He permitted their reform plan, not as an endorsement, but as a mirror. Sometimes, we only learn by eating the fruit we insist on planting.

Saul was chosen as king because he looked the part. Tall, strong, and impressive to the eye. Yet, on coronation day, he hid among the people's suitcases, a telling sign of the baggage that waits wherever we trust in human rulers. Saul lost the kingship almost immediately, preferring self-rule over obedience to God. And a young shepherd named David was anointed king.

Under David's leadership, Israel glimpsed its golden age. He was a poet, a warrior, and worshiper. A man after God's heart. Yet it was not to last. David's lust for power led to adultery, deceit, and the betrayal and murder of a trusted friend.

After David, his son Solomon reigned. He built the temple David longed to construct but could not, because he was a man of fighting and bloodshed. We should probably let the implications of that one settle a bit in what it means for us to build God's house. Solomon was the wisest man who ever lived, but wisdom was not enough. Solomon's heart was divided. The idols of foreign nations, the lure of foreign women, and the pride of empire turned him away as his life ended in futility.

After Solomon, it took mere days for the pride of his son Rehoboam to split the kingdom into a civil war between Israel and Judah (See 1 Kings 12). The one kingdom, ordained to be a lighthouse for all nations to experience the love of God, couldn't even get along with each other.

Kings could not save us.

PROPHETS: PREACHERS CAN'T SAVE US (1 KINGS, ESTHER–EZRA, ISAIAH–MALACHI)

As Israel's story continued, the decline is unmistakable. In Judah, a few kings rose up with hearts to follow God, but most did not. In Israel, nearly every king steered the people further into rebellion. Pride fueled violence. Violence reaped consequences. And the people found themselves in exile. And what did God do? He came low.

Repeatedly, the Father raised up prophets, preachers crying out in the wilderness to call His people home. Often misunderstood, these prophetic messages are filled with poetic complexity and divine ache. Some readers fixate on the judgment texts and harsh indictments, failing to see each book is a unified composition. A single movement of divine music that cannot be understood by cherry-picking a single line. To reduce the prophets to sound bites is like trying to summarize a symphony with a single note.

When you read the prophets as they were meant to be read, this single message rises again and again: The price of our sin is great, but the pursuit of our God is greater.

Consider this refrain from Hosea.

"How can I give you up, O Ephraim?
How can I hand you over, O Israel? …
My heart recoils within me;
my compassion grows warm and tender.
I will not execute my burning anger…
for I am God and not a man,
the Holy One in your midst,
and I will not come in wrath" (Hosea 11:8–9).

Some prophets spoke before the exile, warning of what was coming. Others rose up in the midst of exile, offering hope in the darkness. Still others came after the return from exile, speaking comfort as the people tried to rebuild their lives and land.

In every age, God was faithful to send preachers of hope to them all.

But the hearts of the people remained hardened. The prophets' words brought powerful correction and tender compassion but did little to slow the people's tendency to cling to pride and violence in their crumbling self-made kingdoms.

Preachers couldn't save us.

JOB: AVOIDING SUFFERING CAN'T SAVE US (JOB 1–42)

At the center of the Bible lies wisdom literature, beginning with Job, a story believed by many scholars to be the oldest written or orally preserved book in Scripture. This is fitting, as it reflects the deep ache and enduring questions of the human condition.

Job is introduced as blameless (Job 1:8). He loved God, honored his wife, and was a devoted, praying father. He was wealthy but generous, respected in public, consistent in private, and made a personal promise not to look at a young girl with lust to preserve purity in a culture that cheapened it (Job 31:1). He was the embodiment of integrity.

But something is broken in the story.

An accuser, Satan, prowled the earth, slandering the people God loves. He challenged Job's faithfulness, claiming Job only served God because of His blessings. Then, the bottom fell out. In a single, staggering series of events, Job lost his wealth, his livelihood, and all ten of his children. As he reeled in grief, he's afflicted with unrelenting physical pain. Covered in boils, unable to speak, he sat in silence for a full week.

Job's wife, hardened by grief, counseled her husband to abandon his faith and curse God. And then the rumors started. Surely Job had sinned. Why else would he suffer so deeply?

Several of Job's friends came to his side, and to their credit, they quietly comforted Job for seven days. But when the week was up and Job's misery continued, they quickly made up for lost time. For thirty-five chapters, they argued about suffering, justice, and what Job must have done to bring this upon himself. They demanded confession. He insisted on his innocence. They argued theology. He pleaded for a face-to-face with God.

His story is excruciating. I would argue that much of our own lives are lived in these thirty-five chapters of mystery and debate.

But just then, God appeared from within a whirlwind...and answered none of Job's questions. Instead, He posed His own.

- "Where were you when I laid the earth's foundation?" (Job 38:4).
- "Who shut up the sea behind doors when it burst forth from the womb?" (Job 38:8 NIV)
- "Can you bind the chains of the Pleiades or loosen Orion's belt?" (Job 39:31 NIV).
- "Have you entered the storehouses of the snow or seen the storehouses of the hail?" (Job 38:22 NIV).

It wasn't divine deflection. It was invitation. With every question, God revealed not only His vastness but His nearness. He doesn't explain the mystery—He is the mystery. But He is also good, present, wise, and faithful. It's as if He were saying, "Job, you can't see it all. But I can. And I have good plans, better than you can ask or imagine, if you'd only trust me."

When God finished, He rebuked Job's friends, not for weeping, or doubting, or lamenting, but for misrepresenting both Job's character and God's. They didn't understand the story, so they misread the fruit.

After all this, Job responded. He had finally seen the God with whom he'd demanded an audience. And he did not say, "I've seen a God too severe," or too…angry, or too…scary. Instead, Job confessed, "Surely I spoke of things I did not understand, things too wonderful for me to know.…My ears had heard of you but now my eyes have seen you" (Job 42: 3, 5 NIV).

One glimpse of God was enough. Job's questions dissolved in the light of God's presence. He was safe. He was known. He was held. And he now knew, beyond any doubt, that God was working wonders behind the veil. What did God do in Job's suffering, confusion, and the foolishness of his friends?

He came low.

Not with retribution, but with revelation. Not with wrath but wrapping His arms around His struggling son.

In the end, Job was not only restored, but he also lived a life of multiplied blessings. His story echoes Paul's words centuries later. He wrote, "Our light and momentary afflictions are achieving for us an eternal glory that far outweighs them all" (2 Corinthians 4:17 NIV).

God *will* be better than we imagined in the end. But today, in a world still marked by pride and violence, everything that can be shaken will shake (Hebrews 12:28). Including us. Our obsession to avoid suffering at all costs cannot save us.

ECCLESIASTES: PURSUING PLEASURE CAN'T SAVE US (ECCLESIASTES 1–12)

At one point in history, Solomon held the rare trifecta of human achievement as the wisest man alive, the wealthiest, and the most powerful king over God's chosen people. He was the envy of nations and the winner of every imaginable Most Likely to Succeed superlative.

And so, he did what most people would do if given the means. He set out on a personal reform plan to find meaning in life through anything and everything that promised fulfillment.

The book of Ecclesiastes chronicles his journey. He chased after everything our culture still clings to today—knowledge, pleasure, entertainment, wine, luxury, laughter, sex, success, fame, accomplishment, possessions, and influence (Ecclesiastes 1–5). If it could be consumed or collected, Solomon tried it.

He found all of them without meaning, a vapor unable to satisfy his soul. It all slipped through his fingers. He penned this conclusion: "Now all has been heard; here is the conclusion of the matter: Fear God and keep his commandments, for this is the duty of all mankind" (Ecclesiastes 12:13 NIV).

Solomon believed living his best life would make him happy. And the Father let him try, recording it in the inspired Scriptures so you and I wouldn't have to chase the same empty promises.

Stuff can't save us.

KINGDOM SONGS: (SELAH) A PREVIEW OF THE ONE WHO CAN SAVE US (PSALMS, PROVERBS, SONG OF SOLOMON)

In this final movement of the Old Testament, we're given another selah. A sacred pause to reflect on the God who can save us. In Psalm 1:3, we meet the tree planted by streams of living water. Its leaves stay green, and it produces fruit continually.

Later, we will learn that Jesus is this Vine, the One in whom we will bear much fruit (John 15:1–5). Through sacred poetry and song, we encounter sons and daughters who bring both praise and protest before God, who wrestle with His presence and His silence, yet still come boldly. This is not the God of religion, but a Father who longs for our unfiltered honesty.

In Proverbs 3:5–6, we're invited to build our lives on Wisdom, not our own understanding but hers. Lady Wisdom echoes the Spirit, calling us away from pride and violence to follow God in the way of love. And in Song of Solomon, we glimpse the heart of the Divine as Lover, a relentless pursuer who delights in us, desires us, and draws near to remind our hearts that we are His beloved, and He is our greatest love. (Song of Solomon 6:3).

These are not random poems or moral platitudes. They are a whisper of what's coming. A preview of the One who will not just point us to salvation but be Salvation Himself.

The Old Testament records a God who continually draws near, permitting, providing, and patiently offering reform plans to slow our self-destruction. With every failure, He doesn't retaliate in wrath but reveals more of His unending mercy. He keeps walking the long road of redemption.

In the end, we, like Solomon, have exhausted every possible reform plan. And we have to admit we've come up bankrupt.

The next generation couldn't save us.

Starting over couldn't save us.

Sacrifices couldn't save us.

A nation couldn't save us.

A leader couldn't save us.

Laws couldn't save us.

New surroundings couldn't save us.

Kings couldn't save us.

Preachers couldn't save us.
Avoiding suffering couldn't save us.
Stuff couldn't save us.
The fullness of time had finally come.

DISCUSSION QUESTIONS

1. Paul says *we see in a mirror dimly.* Where have you experienced distortion in how you see God? What helped (or could help) bring clarity to His true nature?
2. This chapter introduces the idea that the Old Testament unfolds in a series of reform plans, not final solutions. Which reform attempt (Cain, Noah, Babel, etc.) resonates with your own story of striving? What does it teach you about God's patience, and about your need for a Rescuer?
3. How did this chapter shift the way you understand God's posture in the Old Testament? Where do you see Him presently *coming low* to rescue you?

SEVEN

"THIS IS MY SON. LISTEN TO HIM."

How all the Law and the Prophets Find Their Fullness in Jesus

OVER THE PAST SEVERAL DECADES, I've had the privilege of teaching the Bible to people from every corner of the social and spiritual spectrum. I've taught believers and skeptics, scholars and seekers, the deeply wounded and the deeply curious. Across all these diverse settings, I've encountered surprising yet consistent challenges. We often attempt to make the Bible answer questions it isn't even trying to address. We approach it like a modern encyclopedia, a science textbook, or a political manifesto, bringing our assumptions to the text in an unconscious attempt to force the story to fit into our pre-formed boxes.

Take Genesis, for example. It wasn't written to explain the moment-by-moment mechanics of creation, or to provide commentary on dinosaurs or the age of the earth. The story it tells is true—but it's a different kind of origin story. It isn't a lab report. It's a love letter.

The Old Testament Laws aren't a rulebook for modern Christians to apply to the letter without context. They were given to the ancient Israelites as a reform plan to help them encounter the God of Jacob as distinct from the violent, manipulative gods of their neighbors. So please, don't quote Leviticus to your teenager about tattoos. That's not what it's saying.

The Old Testament narratives aren't morality stories of heroes and villains. They're stories of broken people just like us grappling with faith, failure, and the need for rescue. The point isn't to become like David or avoid being like Saul. It's that we all need Jesus. *He's* the hero. The rest of us are His rescue mission.

The Psalms aren't just pretty worship songs. They're sacred journal entries. Raw cries from mountaintops and valleys where God's people wrestle honestly with pain, joy, doubt, and hope. Though fully inspired, not all their emotions reflect God's will. When the psalmist cries out, "Happy is the one who seizes your infants and dashes them against the rocks," that's not God's heart, but the heart of a grieving exile venting unfiltered and unhealed rage (see Psalm 137:9). And God in His kindness said, "Put it in the hymnal." Because His grace waits to meet us in the places we're willing to be honest.

The Proverbs aren't divine guarantees. They don't promise that if you parent well your kids will never go astray. They're poetic principles—truisms inviting us to walk the path of wisdom. And Wisdom, ultimately, is a person. His name is Jesus.

The Minor and Major Prophets aren't rants from a moody God. They proclaim the cries of a heartbroken Father warning His children that pride and violence ruin us. In the Prophets, the Father calls us home with tender, relentless love. Again and again, the prophetic books reveal a God who says, "How can I give up on you?" even when we stopped listening.

The Old Testament progressively unveils God's nature. And just like us, the people within its pages, even the most zealous, didn't always understand the story He was telling.

A CASE STUDY: ELIJAH AND THE PROPHETS OF BAAL

Deep in the failed reform of the kings, Israel was a mess. Ahab, their king, was described in 1 Kings 16:30 as the evilest king. None compared to him. He married Jezebel, a foreign queen who led the people to embrace the worship of Baal and Asherah. Baal was the so-called god of rain, wind, and fertility. Asherah, depending on the tradition, was Baal's mother, his lover, or both.[48] (Cue the Jerry Springer theme song.)

The worship of these gods was vile, involving unspeakable rituals, including child sacrifice by fire. With Israel's king leading the nation into this darkness, the people were in grave danger. And what did God do?

He came low.

God called a prophet named Elijah to bring the people back to the one true God (1 Kings 18:37).

Elijah's first duty was to announce a drought. Why? Because the people revered Baal as the god of rain. Just as God had with Pharaoh, He was pleading with Ahab through mercy, not wrath, so he would see the futility of his idolatry and repent. The drought mirrored Ahab and the people's parched hearts, and a call to return to the source of Living Water. Interestingly, Ahab eventually humbled himself. Our God really is that kind.

But before Ahab turned to God, he was furious. He wanted Elijah dead. God protected the prophet, hiding him in a ravine and feeding him by ravens. For three long years, Ahab refused to relent. And still, God was patient. Finally, for the sake of the people, God told Elijah the rain would return.

Ironically, the very moment God called Elijah to reveal himself, Jezebel was on a violent spree to hunt and kill any remaining prophets of Yahweh. So, Elijah stood on Mt. Carmel and issued a challenge before the people. On one side, 450 prophets of Baal stood. On the other, Elijah stood alone, as he called the people to stop wavering between two kingdoms.

Both sides would prepare an offering and call on their god to answer by fire. Whoever answered was the true God.

The prophets of Baal went first. From morning to afternoon, they shouted, danced, and cut themselves, bleeding openly, in a desperate attempt to earn Baal's favor. No one answered. In a humorous exchange, Elijah began to taunt, "Maybe your god is sleeping…or in the bathroom" (1 Kings 18:27 my paraphrase).

Then Elijah rebuilt the altar of the Lord. He drenched it in water three times so no one could accuse him of a trick. Then he prayed a simple twenty-second prayer.

"O Lord, God of Abraham, Isaac, and Israel, let it be known this day that you are God in Israel, and that I am your servant, and that I have done all these things at your word. Answer me, O Lord, answer me, that this people may know that you, O Lord, are God, and that you have turned their hearts back" (1 Kings 18:36b–37).

Fire fell. The people cried out, "The Lord—he is God!" (vs. 39). Then, in a jarring turn, Elijah led the prophets of Baal down to the Kishon Valley and slaughtered all of them.

Years later, we arrive at a very different mountain.

Jesus sent His disciples ahead into a Samaritan village to prepare a place for them, but the people rejected Him. James and John were incensed. Recalling Elijah, they asked, "Lord, do you want us to call down fire from heaven to destroy them?" (Luke 9:54, NIV).

This wasn't a random request. They were standing in the very hills of Samaria where Elijah had called down fire from heaven—not once, but twice (see also 2 Kings 1). The very ground beneath their feet had witnessed it. And now, it seemed, history was about to repeat itself. James and John wished to imitate their spiritual hero, the father of prophets. But Jesus' response should stop us in our tracks.

"But Jesus turned and scolded them. [And Jesus said, 'You don't know what kind of spirit you belong to. The Son of Man did not come to destroy the souls of people but to save them']" (Luke 9:55–56 NCV).

He didn't say, "That worked for Elijah, but this is a different situation." He didn't say, "This is something I used to do, but now we're in a different season." No. He said, "That request comes from a different spirit."

He rebuked them—a word used for silencing demons, storms, and Satan himself. This was not a polite redirection. It was a forceful rejection of a destructive *spirit.* James and John were left reeling. Their entire framework for righteous leadership was upended. Elijah was their hero. But here stood Jesus, God in flesh saying, "You're following the wrong model."

Soon after, Jesus took James and John, along with Peter, to the top of a mountain, where He was transfigured before them. And alongside Him appeared Moses and Elijah, the two men representing the Law and the

Prophets. The pillars of their holy Scriptures. Overwhelmed, Peter thought this marked the perfect occasion to set up tents, roast s'mores and hear campfire stories. He wanted to *tabernacle* in this place with his heroes.

But a voice thundered from a bright cloud.

"'This is my beloved Son, with whom I am well pleased; listen to him'...and when they lifted up their eyes, they saw *no one but Jesus only*" Matthew 17:5, 8 (emphasis mine).

Moses and Elijah were never the main event. Their ministries were shadows. Good shadows. Inspired shadows. But shadows nonetheless. And now, the Light had come.

Sadly, many today defend violent interpretations of the Law and the Prophets, while ignoring the Prophet who came as the very Law of love. They celebrate Elijah's slaughter while silencing the Lamb who was slain to end our need for violence.

They love the vengeance on Mount Carmel but refuse to embody the Beatitudes of the Sermon on the Mount.

Maybe it's time to change what mountain we're standing on.

I don't understand every detail of what Elijah did with his enemies, but I do know what Jesus teaches concerning ours.

"You have heard that it was said, 'You shall love your neighbor and hate your enemy.' But I say to you, Love your enemies and pray for those who persecute you, so that you may be sons of your Father who is in heaven. For he makes his sun rise on the evil and on the good, and sends rain on the just and on the unjust" (Matthew 5:43–45).

"Love your enemies, do good to those who hate you, bless those who curse you, pray for those who abuse you" (Luke 6:27–28).

"Do not repay evil with evil or insult with insult. On the contrary, repay evil with blessing, because to this you were called so that you may inherit a blessing" (1 Peter 3:9 NIV).

"Bless those who persecute you; bless and do not curse them...Repay no one evil for evil, but give thought to do what is honorable in the sight of all. If possible, so far as it depends on you, live peaceably with all" (Romans 12:14, 17–18).

I've caught heat for insinuating Elijah's slaughter of Baal's prophets as anything less than the Christian Super Bowl. I get it. This was once my favorite Bible story to share with my kids.

But here's my dilemma. Jesus was asked His commentary about this exact moment, and He didn't mix words. Perhaps Elijah's actions were warranted for reasons we cannot understand, but we weren't given the mandate to echo Elijah. We are called to follow Jesus.

This is my Son. Listen to Him.

TOOLS TO BETTER UNDERSTAND THE STORY

We've seen how even the most revered stories of Scripture, when held up to the light of Jesus, may carry elements that demand reexamination of how we are called to live. If we are to carry a gospel worthy of Jesus, we need more than selective Bible quotes or inherited interpretations. We need tools to help us understand how our divine Author reveals Himself on every page of Scripture. The rest of this chapter is a practical guide to do just that.

Over the past twenty-five years, I've immersed myself in the languages, cultural settings, and literary devices of the ancient world. One thing is clear. The biblical authors used techniques the original audiences would've immediately understood but modern readers often miss completely. Let's look at a few that can help us better read the written Word, so we can more clearly see the Living Word.

Tool 1: Primary and Secondary Causes and Why *God Sent* May Not Mean What We Think

Ancient Near Eastern cultures were steeped in polytheism, with gods of rain, crops, fertility, and just about everything else. In contrast, Israel declared all things under the dominion of one sovereign God. In doing so, they developed a literary shorthand that attributed every occurrence—rain, sickness, war, blessing—as something *sent by God.*

This isn't because they believed God was micromanaging every lightning bolt like Zeus hurling thunder. It was a theological declaration stating, "Nothing happens apart from His hand."

Ancient writers employed the phrase *God sent* indiscriminately, whether or not God was actively involved in sending something, or if it was a secondary cause of something in the created order that God chose not to interrupt. So, where we would say, "It rained today," they would say, "God opened the heavens." If you searched for a job, filled out an application, and got hired, they would say, "God sent a job." If we saw a cow standing in a field suddenly struck by lightning, they'd say, "God sent fire from the sky and struck the cow."

Why? Because they tried to communicate that nothing in creation was greater than God, and nothing could happen apart from His hand. While true, this often leaves the modern reader thinking God *initiated* something that He only *permitted* in a free-choice, fallen world. Old Testament scholar Walt Kaiser explains, "There is a lack of precise distinction in Hebraic thought between primary and secondary causes. Since God is sovereign, human will and freedom to decide for or against God were often subsumed under divine sovereignty."[49]

Sometimes the phrasing chosen by biblical authors can suggest to modern readers that God directly causes what He only permits, by giving humans free will. At other times, it may seem that God is actively sending punishment, when in reality, people are simply experiencing the consequences of their own choices.

Here are a few examples of what's in the Bible, what the Bible affirms, and what is likely happening.

What the Bible says:

"The next day a harmful spirit from God rushed upon Saul" (1 Samuel 18:10).

What the Bible affirms:

"God cannot be tempted by evil and does not tempt anyone; but each person is tempted when they are dragged away by their own evil desire and enticed. Then, after desire has conceived, it gives birth to sin; and sin, when it is full-grown, gives birth to death" (James 1:13–15 NIV).

What is likely happening:

God rejected Saul as king due to his prideful disobedience. Saul harbored jealousy against David. The Bible is clear that our unrepentant anger gives our enemy a foothold (Ephesians 4:27). When we allow evil desires to incubate and grow within us, nasty things are birthed on earth. Saul's pride led to violence. The statement in the text simply affirms this did not happen apart from God's sovereignty. Let's look at another example.

What the Bible says:

The Lord hardened Pharaoh's heart. (Exodus 9:12)

What the Bible affirms:

"Do I take any pleasure in the death of the wicked?" declares the Sovereign Lord. Rather, am I not pleased when they turn from their ways and live?" (Ezekiel 18:23 NIV).

What is likely happening:

The story alternates between mentioning Pharaoh hardening his own heart and the Lord hardening Pharaoh's heart. That said, the first time the text states the Lord hardened Pharaoh's heart was during the sixth plague. This was after multiple references to Pharaoh hardening his own heart. God doesn't delight in doing anything to cause death. The clear implication is Pharaoh lost all sensitivity, refusing to obey. James wrote about such sin. "After desire has conceived, it gives birth to sin; and sin, when it is full-grown, gives birth to death" (James 1:15 NIV). Yet, Moses desired his readers to know, especially in this showdown between gods, that this wasn't happening apart from the one true God's hand. With a broken heart, God allowed Pharaoh's heart to be hardened.

Tool 2: Sin is Its Own Punishment

Keeping with the idea God sends to humanity, and we ourselves choose, William Paul Young gives a helpful definition. In his best-selling novel, *The Shack*, Young imagines God telling us, "Sin is its own punishment, devouring you from the inside. It's not my purpose to punish it; it's my joy to cure it."[50]

Sin is its own punishment. The nature of sin carries its own painful consequence. It doesn't lead to death because all the fun we're having angers God, so He punishes to make us pay. No. By its very nature, sin brings punishment.

When God patiently warns us concerning the consequences of sin, it's because the nature of sin destroys us.

When we refuse to listen to God's warning and step into sin, we experience the consequences of that sin, not because God is cruel or vindictive, or because He is sending judgment. *It is simply what sin does.*

Here's an analogy. Imagine a man named Hank recovering from a torn ACL, unable to walk or run for six months. Hank, a daredevil, expresses his greatest desire, once he can run again, is to run into the eight-lane expressway outside his house, and try to weave between the cars. Imagine, every day for six months, God comes to sit with Hank and urges him to understand the grave consequences, hoping Hank will relent from his reckless desire to run into traffic. For six months, Hank smiles and nods, but the afternoon he's cleared for physical activity, he bolts straight into the highway and is struck by a speeding car. Hank's friends would be devastated. But no one would think to blame the God who sat with Hank every day for six months, begging him to reconsider. We would recognize Hank's free and foolish decision as his own. Yet this exact scenario, played out in biblical days, would have been recorded as, *And God sent a car to strike Hank and he died.* This is what we mean by a lack of distinction between primary and secondary causes. When we encounter a confusing passage stating *God sent*, and it doesn't seem in line with His character to initiate such a calamity, it's essential to step back and study the full context of the passage and its place within the overall narrative of the biblical story.

Tool 3: "When faced with what you don't know, stand on what you do!"

Brian Zahnd suggests we have three possible ways we can respond to the difficult parts of the Bible that don't seem to align with the God revealed in Jesus.

1. Question God's morality. Perhaps God is, at times, monstrous.
2. Question the immutability of God. Maybe God has changed.

3. Question how we are reading the Bible.[51]

This chapter aims at the third option, not deconstructing Scripture, but returning to the ancient path Jesus offered on the road to Emmaus. And consequently, to the early church fathers' understanding of the non-violent nature of the gospel before Christianity wed itself with the Roman Empire in 313 CE.[52] Parts of the Bible will still puzzle or even trouble you. It's okay to be honest about these questions and to wrestle through them. I do. True faith is only forged in a refiner's fire. Those who seek God as He truly is always find Him there. Don't forget, we haven't arrived. We're still traveling down the dusty trail with Jesus. So, here's what we can do. When faced with something we *don't* know, stand on what we *do*.

We can build our entire spiritual house on the foundation of *the God revealed on the cross*. Jesus Christ incarnate, crucified, and resurrected. We can join Paul in choosing to know nothing "except Jesus Christ and him crucified" (1 Corinthians 2:2 NIV).

Jesus is the Father's message to us.

Jesus is perfect theology.

Whenever we are confused in the shadow of the Old Covenant, we only need to look to the substance of Jesus and ask, "What am I absolutely convinced is the true revealed nature of my God?" You'll be surprised how many places you immediately see what a passage *can't* be saying.

Tool 4: Proof-Texting versus Narrative Tracking

One of the most damaging habits in biblical interpretation is proof-texting—using isolated verses to build a case for pre-decided ideas. It's the theological version of confirmation bias. A better way to interpret Bible passages is what I call narrative tracking. It's reading every passage in the larger context of the whole story, looking patiently for what God is trying to tell us.

I am often asked, "If God is good, then why didn't He explicitly condemn things in the Old Testament like slavery or polygamy?" But this reveals how little we understand about the kind of story God is telling.

In ancient literature, we are expected to know the merit or horror of an action by the fruit it produces. God's will becomes clear by *where the story leads the people.* When reading the Bible, we would greatly benefit to ask several questions.

- "Where is the story headed?"
- "How is it pointing to Jesus and our need for Him?"
- "Is it glorifying wickedness, or is it a glaring warning of where this path leads, so we will avoid it?"
- "Is it ultimately moving us *toward* violence or *away* from it?"

When we read Old Testament passages that mention slavery and polygamy, it's easy to see the futility, brutality, and heartbreak it causes. When Abram sleeps with Hagar and the house erupts in chaos and heartbreak, we're supposed to say, "Yeah, that didn't work."

The Bible doesn't simply tell you something is bad. Often it shows you in the life of a brother or sister.

WHAT THE LIGHT REVEALS IN THE SHADOWS

Shadows in my room looked like monsters until I turned on the light and saw it was just a jacket on a chair. When we read the Old Testament *without the light of Jesus*, we're likely to misidentify God's heart. It might look monstrous. But everywhere the light of the gospel illumines the pages, we begin to see what's really in front of us.

You may still wrestle with some hard passages. That's okay. I do too. We don't have to have all the answers. But as we wrestle, we can keep our eyes on Jesus. We don't have to get lost in the shadows. We can look to the Light…*and listen to the Son.*

DISCUSSION QUESTIONS

1. Have you struggled with a portrait of God in Scripture that felt at odds with the Jesus you know? How did you respond?

2. In your spiritual journey, have you had moments when you were like James and John, zealous for what you thought was "righteous," but later discovered it wasn't Christ's heart? What changed your perspective?
3. What are some ways we might be unknowingly *building tents* for ideas, theologies, or cultural values we've elevated to the same level as Jesus? What does it look like to see Jesus only in those places?

EIGHT

MISSING THE MARK AND MISSING THE POINT

How Jesus fulfilled the Law and completely changed the way we see

IN MAY OF 2002, MY THEN-FIANCÉ, Jill, and I packed a lifetime of milestones into three weekends. We graduated college, got married, and moved two states away to start a brand-new adventure. We were newlyweds in a new city, discovering the beauty of independence and the joy of life together. We were inseparable.

A few months in, Jill made her first out-of-town trip for grad school. The night before she left, I had a dream. Now, most of my dreams are bizarre such as walking through a house made of pizza or talking to a friend who suddenly morphs into a dolphin. But this dream was different. It felt real. I could see the sunlight beaming through the bedroom window, tiny flecks of dust floating in the air. Jill's side of the bed was empty. Missing her already, I reached for her pillow, when suddenly, something invisible grabbed my hand.

I snapped awake to a pitch-black room, completely disoriented. In my sleep, I had in reality reached over, and Jill gently placed her hand on mine. *Only I didn't know that.* My heart raced. My instincts kicked in. I broke my captor's grasp and shouted into the darkness, "Who are you…Who are you?"

Imagine my surprise when I heard the terrified voice of my wife answering back. After a long pause, and some very nervous giggling, we left the TV on for the rest of the night. We laugh about it now, but in these early months of marriage, Jill must have wondered if she'd married a lunatic. I, on the other hand, tried to calm myself from the fight or flight response that overtook me when I'd lovingly reached for the love of my life but encountered a monster in the dark. I think many of us have lived in the tension of the same survival mechanism in our relationship with God for far too long.

MISSING THE MARK

The word *sin* means to miss the mark. A tragic image of a life traveling away from the target we were created to hit.[53] By the end of the Old Testament, it's clear. Humanity missed it. God made us for intimacy, but we chose independence. We were designed to reign with God in love but instead found ourselves enslaved by pride that boiled over into violence, no matter how many reform plans we sought to right the ship.

Musician Eric Clapton once captured the contradiction inside the human heart when he said, "I'm an egomaniac with an inferiority complex!"[54]

This describes all of us somewhere in our lives, self-obsession with an orphan spirit. Wandering. Striving. Terrified there won't be enough love, security, or blessing to go around. Pride is dangerous enough. But when orphan-hearted pride finds itself in power? It becomes a breeding ground for tyrants and terrorists. Kings and queens bent on expanding their own little empires, throwing their weight around in the name of manifest destiny.

Eden's fall fractured the human spirit. Pride replaced presence. Violence replaced vulnerability. And still, the mercy of God kept coming low, slowing our self-destruction, revealing His heart, inviting us back to the life we were always meant to live. But the more His kindness elevated us, the more we used our privileged position to build the wrong kingdom. Time after time He came to His beloved children who missed the mark, and we largely missed the point.

Thinking we were awake in the light, we mistook His embrace for a monster in the dark.

But then...*Jesus came to town.*

THE WHOLE WORLD IS GOING AFTER HIM!

From the very start of His ministry, the religious leaders didn't know what to do with Jesus. He was a rabbi, but He refused to play by their rules or fit into any of their political or religious molds. Meanwhile, the people they ignored, tax collectors, sinners, common fishermen, women, and children, couldn't get enough of Him.

Whenever Jesus entered a town, crowds surged to meet Him. They packed the streets just to hear Him teach or brush against Him in passing. On more than one occasion, Jesus had to preach from a boat pushed out into the lake, the shoreline swarming with hungry hearts. What was it about Jesus they couldn't find anywhere else?

To be with Jesus was to be seen, to be known, to be loved.

Over and over, people found their hearts ignited by His compassion. He knew how to talk to them, but even more, He spoke with authority (Matthew 7:29). Unlike the scribes and experts, Jesus didn't sound like someone quoting God. He sounded like someone who knew Him. His teaching had gravity—it rang true. Reality itself bent toward His words.

And when He reached out His hands to the broken, people were healed. The blind. The deaf. The unclean. The untouchable. Even the dead. To be with Jesus was to be astonished. Unless, of course, you were one of the guardians of the Law. The Pharisees, Sadducees, and scribes clashed with Jesus in nearly every city. The more He taught about His Father, the more they objected. They tried to trap Him with clever questions, discredit Him in front of the crowds, and silence Him with threats. When that didn't work, they plotted to kill Him. Why? Because Jesus didn't merely interpret the Old Testament differently. He embodied it in a way they found dangerous. And He dealt with the Law in a manner so radically unexpected, it seemed blasphemous.

The following cannot be overstated. Jesus, the perfect image of the

Father, taught and revealed the Old Testament in a way the religious establishment deemed worthy of death.

So, what exactly did He say that was so threatening?

THE NEW MOSES, THE TRUE LAW

At the launch of Jesus public ministry, He delivered the longest recorded public address He would ever speak. Known as the Sermon on the Mount, it is considered by many scholars as the New Law—not abolishing the Old but *fulfilling* it in ways no one expected.

Many Christians can quote portions of it, especially familiar lines like "Our Father in heaven…" But few recognize how revolutionary and scandalous it is. For the religious leaders of His day, it was nothing short of a theological earthquake.

THE BEATITUDES: WHO THE FATHER BLESSES

When God created humanity in Genesis, the very first thing He did was bless them (Genesis 1:28). And not from a distance. The word *bless* means to come down from a high place to a low one, to lift the head, meet the eyes, delight in someone, and provide them with everything needed for the road ahead.[55] That's what is meant by the Father's blessing.

And so, when Jesus began His ministry, He began the same way His Father had. Breathing a blessing. That's what the word *beatitude* means. Most of human history is written like a winner's script favoring the rich, powerful, and influential, while pushing the rest to the edges. That's the story of every empire, the unspoken rule of the way things were. These are the things the world says will satisfy our souls and bless us. But in just a few sentences, Jesus flipped it all upside down when He said…

"Blessed are the poor in spirit…"

To be poor in spirit is to know you're spiritually bankrupt—no credentials, no résumé, no fallback plan, completely reliant on God's kindness.[56] Unlike the religious elite who thanked God they were not like other people, the poor in spirit knew their need for God's mercy (see Luke 18:11). Luke's gospel simply says, *the poor,* reminding us the kingdom doesn't shame neediness. It honors it. Jesus came first to tell us that our Father draws near to those who feel bankrupt or powerless, to supremely satisfy their hearts (Psalm 132:15).

"Blessed are those who mourn..."

To mourn is to grieve deeply for something you loved.[57] You might mourn a relationship, a dream, a life. Jesus wasn't calling us to wallow in self-pity but was comforting those who dared to love deeply enough to be broken. The religious system had little room for lament, often equating suffering with sin. To this, Jesus tenderly assured every grieving heart they would know the embrace of the Comforter, one of His favorite titles for Holy Spirit (John 14:26). In His kingdom, we keep loving, even when it hurts, and we don't rush past sorrow. We carry each other *through* it.

"Blessed are the meek..."

Meekness isn't weakness. It's power harnessed by gentle humility.[58] In a world obsessed with using violence to defend our rights, our voice, and our land, the meek lay down their weapons and trust God to defend and provide. In a world where rulers climb ladders built on the backs of others, Jesus says the earth belongs to those who choose and honor gentleness.

"Blessed are those who hunger and thirst for righteousness..."

Righteousness isn't about religious performance. It's a longing for the world to be made right and return to what we were created to be.[59] The deepest hunger of the human heart isn't for comfort, success, or recognition. It's for *Him.* There isn't any other empire worth building or prize worth chasing. He is the treasure in a field worth selling everything to own (Matthew 13:44). And Jesus promises, every heart that hungers for *Him* will be satisfied with the fullness of God Himself.

"Blessed are the merciful..."

Mercy is more than withholding judgment. Mercy shows up with compassion that refuses to weaponize someone's past against them. It comes low to help people in their time of pain.[60] We exercise mercy every time we forgive. We practice it whenever we refuse to judge the motive of someone's heart or the deserved consequences for their actions. Moved by the love of God, we simply help them. Mercy is the opposite of self-righteousness.

Jesus taught that the merciful will receive mercy. Not as a transaction, but because passageways of their hearts open wide to both give and receive grace freely.

"Blessed are the pure in heart..."

The pure in heart posture their souls to be refined by fire.[61] They come close with faith like a child (Matthew 18:3). The pure in heart never believe they've arrived anywhere except into the arms where grace presently holds them. They walk with soft hearts and thick skin. They believe their God works in all things for their good, even trials, and He can be trusted.

Jesus announced the kingdom belongs to those who don't judge the growth of others. They don't look at their brother's faults, because they focus on the Father and where He is working to mature their own hearts. Jesus promised these sons and daughters will see God clearly.

"Blessed are the peacemakers..."

Peacemaker means one who produces peace.[62] These sons and daughters don't merely love peace. No. They posture their lives to reproduce peace in every space they occupy. There is a vast difference between peacemaking and peacekeeping. Peacekeepers avoid conflict at all costs while peacemakers wade into conflict, not to dominate, but to heal. Peacekeepers strive to protect their reputation, but peacemakers are willing to be misunderstood. Peacekeepers work to keep up appearances and to preserve the status quo. Peacemakers courageously step into any space where peace is not presently reigning, and they camp with God in that place until peace is birthed.

To walk as a peacemaker is at the very core of what it means to be a child of God.

"Blessed are those who are persecuted for righteousness..."

Jesus ends His sermon with a gut punch. Said in my own words, "If you live this way, it will cost you. If you hunger for righteousness, show mercy to the undeserving, make peace where others demand payback, and stand for love in the face of hate, you'll be misunderstood, opposed, even rejected." But that's what it means to love. This is love:

- When we refuse to withhold goodness even when we're treated badly...
- When we keep doing the right thing even as we're being wronged...
- When we won't stop blessing in the face of cursing...
- When we don't let the opposition around us change the fruit that is coming out of us...

When we choose to live this way, we look like our Father bearing a love that transcends circumstance or opinions. This is indeed a blessed life. Jesus didn't just give a new list of moral behaviors. He redefined how we see blessing.

This kingdom isn't about power, privilege, or preservation. It's about emptying ourselves so others may be filled with the overflow of the love of God we are experiencing. It is laying down rights so others might rise. Undergirding the overlooked and welcoming in the outcast. Love means choosing to "honor one another above yourselves"

(Romans 12:10). The religious elite of Jesus' day refused to understand this concept. This made Jesus dangerous.

And He was just getting started.

LIGHTHOUSES OF HOPE

As Jesus turned to speak about the Father's calling for His people, He delivered a statement that would have stunned His audience. He told them, "*You* are the light of the world…let *your* light shine before others, so that they may see *your* good works and give glory to *your* Father in heaven" Matthew 5:14, 16 (emphasis added).

Hundreds of years earlier, the prophet Isaiah wrote about the Messiah coming as the light for the Gentiles, but this was different (see Isaiah 49:6 NIV). Jesus later declared Himself as the *Light of the world*, but first He extended the invitation to His followers (see John 8:12). Somehow, as we walk with Him, we are the light of the world too. Before announcing His role, He named ours. We are called to carry the love of God beyond our borders, beyond our comfort zones, beyond the walls of religion, to the nations.

This was the original heart behind the call of Abraham. It was also the reason Moses stood before Pharoah. And now, through Jesus, it came full circle. We are living lighthouses, illuminating the darkness so the wayward can find their way home.

Notice the absence of us versus them in Jesus' words. That contrast couldn't be sharper from the religious system of His day, which prioritized separation from sinners. But Jesus offered something altogether different. He proclaimed a kingdom that doesn't retreat from darkness but radiates light in the middle of the darkness. The light draws in the outsider, welcomes the wanderer, and makes the love of the Father visible to the watching world.

NOT TO ABOLISH THE LAW, BUT TO FULFILL IT

As Jesus stood on the mountain, unpacking the deeper meaning of

God's Law, no one in the crowd could miss the gravity of the moment. He was clearly positioning Himself as a New Moses but with an authority that transcended even Sinai. He wasn't merely interpreting the Law. He was revealing its truest form.

Jesus made it clear. He had not come to abolish the Law, but to fulfill it. He wasn't discarding what came before, but completing it, bringing clarity to the shadows, permanence to the temporary, and a living breath to what was etched in stone. What the Law could only hint at, Jesus embodied. What it demanded, He accomplished. And now, He was unveiling the universal Law of the Father's heart. A law not carved into tablets but written into the hearts of His people. Just as He promised in Jeremiah 31:33.

"YOU HAVE HEARD IT SAID..."

In the next section of Jesus sermon, He directly confronts the legal loopholes that allowed people to weaponize the Law of Moses. He dismantles the ways pride cloaked itself in piety and exposed how the Law was used to justify violence, oppression, and selfishness. But Jesus wasn't delivering something new. He was unveiling what had always been true, what had always been the Father's heart.

Jesus didn't come to eradicate the Law, but to complete it (Matthew 5:17). He came to bring its meaning into full view, and to correct the distorted applications accumulated over generations. His words ask them, and us, to face a difficult truth. We humans have a terrible habit of missing the point. Over time, the Law had become less a reflection of God's design and more a mirror of our hardened hearts.

Jesus addresses six key laws in the Sermon on the Mount. In the first two, He clarifies the intent behind them, deepening their meaning to guard against pride and promote self-emptying love. But in the remaining four, He does something even more radical. He overturns their common understanding entirely. He reveals what was long accepted as the will of God as a shadow, sometimes even a concession, meant to slow our self-destruction until we were ready to see clearly.

This raises a crucial question. If God is unchanging and His Word is inspired, what are we to make of Jesus correcting Old Testament laws?

There are only two possibilities.

1. Moses misunderstood or miscommunicated the Law God intended.
2. The Law was inspired, but given as a temporary, partial measure of God's heart because the people's hearts were not ready for the fullness of God's self-giving love.

As someone who deeply affirms the full inspiration of Scripture, I am convinced it is the second. And if this feels unsettling, hold tight. Jesus Himself explains that certain Old Testament commands were given, not as fixed ideals, but as temporary permissions God granted because of the hardness of human hearts. He starts with a biggie.

Murder

"*You have heard* that it was said to the people long ago, 'You shall not murder; and anyone who murders will be subjuct to judgment.' *But I tell you* that anyone who is angry with a brother or sister will be subject to judgment. Again, anyone who says to a brother or sister, 'Raca,' is answerable to the court. And anyone who says, 'You fool!' will be in danger of the fire of hell" (Matthew 5:21–22 NIV, emphasis added).

This was one of the clearest commands in the Law. It was the sixth of the Ten Commandments in Exodus 20:13, commanding, "Do not murder." Case closed, right? Not quite. Jesus quotes it and then adds a disruptive phrase, "But I say to you…" They believed they grasped the full will of God, but in this moment, Jesus redefines their interpretation of the inspired Law. Remember, the Bible is inspired. Our interpretation is not. Here, Jesus digs deeper, beyond *external action* to *internal intent.*

Let's follow His progression. Anger makes one guilty before God. (This word means provoked rage.)[63]

Raca requires further accountability before the community at the hands of the Sanhedrin. (Raca was an Aramaic slur calling someone empty or worthless.)[64] But calling someone foolish or stupid places them in danger of *Gehenna*, a term often translated as hell in English translations.

What is happening here?

Jesus reverses the order we expect. He begins with murder, the gravest offense, yet reserves the strongest warnings for what we might consider lesser sins, like name-calling, devaluing, and dismissing. Why?

Because Jesus is not pruning branches. He's pulling up roots.

Murder doesn't begin with a weapon. It begins in the heart, with pride that inflates self and diminishes others. Before a hand ever strikes, the heart has already judged, dismissed, and dehumanized. The root system Jesus is targeting is our hidden pride that grows into a toxic violence. This is what poisons our relationships and desecrates the image of God in our neighbor.

Those listening would have been speechless, assuming Jesus added something new to this law. But Jesus isn't adding anything. He's removing a veil so we can see what righteousness in the kingdom of heaven has always looked like. Jesus is taking off the training wheels of the Mosaic Law that people had used to rank their worth and shame others. And He is doing this hoping we will realize we can't do it in our own power. All of us, in our own effort, fall short of the law of murder, killing a great many in our hearts every day.

But here's the hope. We aren't called to fulfill the Law. Jesus came to fulfill it for us, giving us a new heart able to seek His kingdom in the way of peace.

God's standard didn't change. It's our understanding that must mature. He invites us to see a fuller picture of His unchanged heart. The Law commanded, Don't take life. But Jesus gives the fuller command, "Give life. Protect life. Honor life. Even in your heart." True righteousness isn't merely avoiding bloodshed. It's refusing contempt. It's loving without rage, judgment, or violence. This is self-emptying love. And the kingdom grows only in this soil. But Jesus doesn't stop there. He continues with another painful topic.

Adultery

"*You have heard* that it was said, 'You shall not commit adultery.' *But*

I say to you that everyone who looks at a woman with lustful intent has already committed adultery with her in his heart" (Matthew 5:27–28, emphasis added).

Once again, Jesus referenced one of the Ten Commandments—this time, the call to marital faithfulness in Exodus 20:14. For most, the law was reduced to a simple boundary. Don't physically betray your spouse. But Jesus wasn't just drawing the line farther back. He was illuminating the whole heart of the matter.

To *lust* means to harbor a forbidden desire.[65] It means to use another person, even in thought, to gratify ourselves. In a culture that condoned a thousand variations of *look, but don't touch*, Jesus exposed how shallow and self-serving that kind of thinking was. The Father never gave marriage merely to keep us from cheating. He gave it as a sacred covenant of intimacy, friendship, communion, and mutual self-giving.

Jesus declared that to reduce another person, especially one who was not your spouse, to a sexual object in your imagination is an act of inward violence. It robs them of dignity. It violates the trust of your spouse. And it corrodes the covenant you were created to embody. In the kingdom of God, love doesn't take. It gives. It doesn't devour. It delights.

True fidelity means offering your whole self—eyes, thoughts, imagination, body, and heart to the one you've vowed to love. Anything less distorts the gift and misses the mark of the Father's heart. That brings us to Jesus' next teaching on marriage.

Divorce

"*It has been said,* 'Anyone who divorces his wife must give her a certificate of divorce.' *But I tell you* that anyone who divorces his wife, except for sexual immorality, makes her the victim of adultery, and anyone who marries a divorced woman commits adultery" (Matthew 5:31–32 NIV, emphasis added).

Jesus referenced a law from Deuteronomy 24, originally given to protect women during a very specific phase of the Jewish betrothal process. In ancient Israel, marriage unfolded in stages. It began with a legal betrothal, when vows were exchanged and a bride price was paid. Later came the consummation, when the groom returned with a home prepared for his bride. In the time between, a husband who suspected unfaithfulness could issue a certificate of divorce. This was why Joseph considered divorcing Mary. Though they had not yet consummated their marriage, it was a legally binding union.

Over time, this divorce law became grossly distorted. Men used it as a loophole to discard their wives for almost any reason. In fact, there was even a teaching from the Jewish Mishnah that instructed men they could divorce their wives for spoiling a dish, or if they found another woman more attractive.[66] In a patriarchal society where women had few rights, this left many women socially shamed, economically abandoned, and relationally disqualified. What began as a provision for protection became permission for exploitation.

And what did Jesus do? He stepped in and shut it down.

In one sentence, Jesus confronted the systemic mistreatment of women and reclaimed the sacred dignity of marriage. This wasn't a tweak to the law—it was a full course correction. It's as if Jesus was saying, "You've taught you can divorce your wife for any reason. But I tell you, that was never the Father's heart."

Later, when questioned by the Pharisees, Jesus went past Moses straight to Eden when He said, "Moses *permitted* you to divorce your wives because your hearts were hard. *But it was not this way from the beginning*" (Matthew 19:8, NIV emphasis added).

This moment is profound. Jesus acknowledges that Moses permitted something God never commanded. Why? Because their hearts weren't ready. The law was inspired, but not as the final word. It was a speed bump to slow their destruction, a compass meant to guide them away from the cruelty of surrounding cultures and toward the heart of the Father. Just as a parent gives age-appropriate wisdom to their child, God revealed His heart progressively, only as much as He knew His children were ready to receive.

Let me be clear. The Old Testament Law was a gift. It was God-breathed. It was good. But it was never intended to be the universal and sufficient stand-alone revelation of God's will for all people, for all time. As Paul wrote, "No one can be made right with God by following the law. The law only shows us our sin" (Romans 3:20 NCV).

This has always been God's pattern. *He comes low*, meets us in our mess, and reveals as much of His heart as we are willing to receive. Theologian Greg Boyd says it this way, "God has always revealed his true character and will as much as possible while stooping to accommodate the fallen and culturally conditioned state of his people as much as necessary."[67]

I've seen this play out in my parenting. From the time my son Bradley was a baby, I dreamed of his future, leaning in to help shape his calling and character. But I didn't develop flashcards of colleges, jobs, or a future spouse when he was a baby. I simply *stayed present* in the moment celebrating his first steps, cheering when he could pour his own cereal, applauding the first time he mowed the lawn like he'd conquered the world.

Good fathers lead patiently, *right where their kids are*. They don't overwhelm them with what they can't yet carry. They walk with them through every advance and setback, until their child is ready to step into the life that was always waiting.

I believe God is like that.

So, why did God allow certain concessions in the Old Testament? Because His children were still spiritual toddlers, surrounded by brutal cultures and foreign gods. Israel's civil law was revolutionary for its time. It protected women, the poor, foreigners, and the oppressed in ways the world had never seen. But they were just learning how to walk.

And, as they did, I imagine they felt like they conquered the world. But somewhere along the way, they weaponized the Law, confusing God's patient instruction with His permanent intention.

They used God's reforms as tools for pride and instruments of violence.

But the Law was never meant to save us. It was never the finish line. They were training wheels. Shadows. A waypoint on the journey.

In the fullness of time, Jesus came not to create loopholes, but to give us the capacity to love. Because the real solution was never better rules but brand-new hearts. Hearts that honor marriage, not as a contract to manage or dissolve, but as a covenant to cherish and so reflect His love for His Church.

We need to make one crucial clarification. This passage was never intended as a hammer of condemnation for those who've walked through the pain of divorce. Jesus doesn't shame the wounded. He heals them. And every divorced person I've ever spoken with confirms what Jesus said. Divorce feels like trying to separate one person into two. It tears, wounds, and aches. Jesus isn't dismissing that pain.

His goal here wasn't condemnation, but protection. He came to end the subjugation of women, elevate marriage as sacred, and call both husbands and wives into a self-emptying love that mirrors His own (see Ephesians 5:25).

Promises

"Again, *you have heard that it was said* to the people long ago, 'Do not break your oath, but fulfill to the Lord the vows you have made.' *But I tell you,* do not swear an oath at all...all you need to say is simply 'Yes' or 'No'; anything beyond this comes from the evil one" (Matthew 5:33–37 NIV, emphasis added).

Here, Jesus was referencing a law from the book of Numbers. It said, "If a man vows a vow to the Lord, or swears an oath to bind himself by a pledge, he shall not break his word. He shall do according to all that proceeds out of his mouth" (Numbers 30:2).

Here was the problem. The people had turned the law into a loophole. They were making rash and manipulative promises then insisting they had to follow through because they had done it in God's name.

It was circular reasoning at its worst, and it led to one of the most tragic stories in Scripture. A man named Jephthah, born out of wedlock and rejected by his brothers, was recruited to lead Israel into battle against the Ammonites. In a desperate bid for victory and status, he made a reckless vow to God saying, "If you will give the Ammonites into my hand, then whatever comes out from the doors of my house to meet me when I return in peace from the Ammonites shall be the Lord's, and I will offer it up for a burnt offering" (Judges 11:30–31).

Jephthah wins the battle and returns home, only to be greeted by his daughter dancing with joy. What follows is chilling. Jephthah, clinging to a twisted sense of duty, laments to his daughter he cannot break his vow (Judges 11:35). After two months of mourning, she returned, and Jephthah did to her as he vowed.

This is not presented as a tale of honor, but a horror story, violence dressed up in sacred robes. This tragedy is meant to shake us from following in Jephthah's footsteps.

In Jesus' day, the Pharisees were doing something equally manipulative. Though God commanded them to care for their aging parents, they created a legal workaround. If they vowed their money as dedicated to God, they could justify withholding help from their own family in the name of holy service (Mark 7:11–13).

And Jesus had enough.

He stood before the crowds and said plainly, "Let your yes mean yes, and your no mean no." In other words, stop invoking God to sanctify your self-interest. Just be honest. Be trustworthy. Be people whose integrity is so evident that oaths aren't necessary.

Once again, Jesus wasn't discarding the Law. He was fulfilling it by pointing us to the only One whose word is always yes and amen (1 Corinthians 1:20). In doing so, He pulled off the religious disguises that paraded hypocrisy like a badge of honor. And if that wasn't unsettling enough, His next words would land like a punch to the gut. The irony? Just as they braced to defend their right to retribution, Jesus removed it entirely commanding them, instead, to turn the other cheek.

Revenge

"*You have heard that it was said,* 'An eye for an eye, and a tooth for a tooth.' *But I say to you,* do not resist the one who is evil. But if anyone slaps you on the right cheek, turn to him the other also" (Matthew 5:38–39, emphasis added).

The law of retaliation, *lex talionis*, appears three times in the Old Testament.[68] Originally, it served as a civil code for ancient Israel, a temporary reform to restrain unchecked violence and protect the vulnerable by ensuring justice was proportional to the offense.

But by Jesus' day, lex talionis had been hijacked. What was once a protection became a personal weapon. Religious leaders and everyday citizens alike wielded it to justify revenge in even the pettiest of disputes. It was martial law in the name of God.

And so, Jesus did what He always does. He went deeper.

He revealed that this law was also a *concession*, an accommodation for hard hearts, not a final revelation of the Father's will. The true heart of God had never been about retaliation. It was, and has always been, about restoration. About love.

So, Jesus taught to love your enemies.

- Do not or take a defensive stance toward those who wrong you.[69]
- If someone strikes your cheek, physically or with insult, offer the other.
- If someone sues you for your shirt, give them your coat as well.
- If they force you to walk a mile, as Roman soldiers could legally do, walk two.
- If someone asks something of you, give freely.

This wasn't a call to become a doormat. It was a radical return to Eden.

Remember, the context concerns our rights to take revenge when wronged. In Christ, we are not eye for an eye people. In a world obsessed with getting even, we are becoming a people of blessing.

To follow Jesus is to lay down the sword of retaliation and pick up the cross of love. This was Jesus' next topic.

Love

"*You have heard that it was said,* 'Love your neighbor and hate your enemy.' *But I tell you,* love your enemies and pray for those who persecute you, that you may be children of your Father in heaven" (Matthew 5:43–45 NIV, emphasis added).

With His final teaching in this section, Jesus struck at the very heart of the gospel. Love. The kind of love that fulfills the whole Law (Matthew 22:36–40). The kind of love that makes us look just like our Father.

But first, Jesus did something shocking. He quoted a command that didn't exist anywhere in Scripture. He said, "You have heard…'Hate your enemy.'"

But you won't find that verse. In fact, the opposite is true. The Law commands, "Do not seek revenge or bear a grudge" (Leviticus 19:18 NIV). And Proverbs go on to state, If your enemy is hungry, feed him (Proverbs 25:21). So, where did religious leaders get the idea that God was okay with enemy-hating?

Around 100 BC, a sect of separatist religious leaders referred to themselves as the Sons of Light. They believed holiness came through total separation from those deemed impure or unworthy. One of their foundational texts, the *Community Rule*, made their position unmistakably clear. It read, "They may love all the sons of light…and hate all the sons of darkness."[70]

By the time Jesus arrived, this mindset had so thoroughly seeped into the religious atmosphere, the teachers taught it as if it were inspired Law.

Selective hearing is the breeding ground of spiritual empires. In every generation, pride amplifies the theologies that serve its ambitions and mutes the prophets who call us to repent. But Jesus in Matthew 12:33 reminds us, "The tree is known by its fruit."

And the fruit of enemy-hating-religion always looks and tastes the same—violence, division, and the slow death of compassion.

Jesus came to uproot it all.

He didn't just call for tolerance. He commanded love. A love that prays for enemies and embraces outsiders. A love that pursues with unflinching devotion and breaks the cycle of vengeance with the mercy of our Father.

This kind of love reveals whose children we really are.

NO MONSTER IN THE DARK

Here's the truth. We couldn't fulfill the Law.

We couldn't shake the pride that birthed a million forms of violence. We couldn't silence the judgment festering on the inside or the rage erupting on the outside. We couldn't be faithful with our eyes, our thoughts, or our bodies. Nor could we cherish covenant, trading matrimony for manipulation.

We couldn't stop making promises we wouldn't keep. And we couldn't make peace. We ran from God, warred with our neighbor, and condemned the soul staring back at us in the mirror. Though we'd been made by Love and for Love, we couldn't figure out how to live there for the life of us.

The Law couldn't save us. It was never meant to.

We needed a Rescuer not a warlord leading another human revolution. We needed a Deliverer who would crush the serpent and reclaim our inheritance through costly, self-emptying love, not a bloody conquest.

He was no monster in the dark but a light in the darkness.

The Light of the World.

And His name is Jesus.

DISCUSSION QUESTIONS

1. Jesus called His followers to be light to the world. What does it look like for us, as individuals and a community, to embody that kind of light in our culture?
2. Which of Jesus' clarifications in the Sermon on the Mount (e.g., anger, lust, divorce, retaliation, enemy love) most challenges your heart right now? Why do you think that is?
3. The Pharisees used the Law to build systems of pride and exclusion. What are some ways modern Christians might fall into similar traps today?

NINE

GOD IS NOT THE GODFATHER

Seeing the judgment of God through the eyes of Christ

AT NINETEEN, I BECAME a part-time youth pastor at a small Baptist church in a town whose claim to fame was a gas station/bar combo called the Neon Cowboy. Yes, you read that last sentence correctly. I look back on those early ministry days with a blend of gratitude, humility, and about a thousand "What was I thinking?" moments. So many things went wrong. During an outreach night, a middle schooler walked onstage behind me, mid-sermon, proudly flipping off every person in attendance. Once, an underage teen stole my car for an unauthorized joyride. One night, during a disastrously planned lock-in game, a student found himself duct-taped midair to the pristine drywall of our brand-new fellowship hall. When his breathing was unexpectedly restricted, our frantic rescue left behind a human-shaped crater that shouted, "Youth ministry happened here!"

But the evening I loaded a van full of teenagers to attend a local production of *Heaven's Gates, Hell's Flames* topped the list. If you've never seen it, imagine walking into a megachurch for a low-budget, high-drama spectacle portraying what supposedly happens the moment you die. For ninety minutes, a rotating cast of adults, teens, and kids act out scenes of death, judgment, and salvation. In each vignette, a Christian pleads with a friend, co-worker, or relative to accept Jesus and get their name in the Book of Life. Predictably, the person they're trying to convince scoffs or delays, only to die moments later in a car crash, overdose, gang shooting, or freak accident.

Then comes the split-screen judgment. On one side, a glowing staircase to heaven with the *Hallelujah Chorus* booming as the believer is welcomed by an angel, name-checked, and embraced by a toga-clad Jesus. Cue applause. On the other side is a red strobe, fog machine, and a low demonic drone as the unbeliever tries to run toward Jesus. Angels with sickles block his entry, as they drag him screaming into hell. In one particularly traumatic scene, a mother is pulled offstage by her ankles while her daughter begs Jesus for just one more chance to save her. I wish I were exaggerating.

After the final scene, the lights come up, a pastor steps forward, and with ominous warning says, "You don't know what's going to happen when you walk out that door." Dozens of teens and adults flood the altar in tears. This play was billed as a major win for the gospel.

But what gospel won them?

Was heaven intended to be populated by the fear of hell or by the beauty of Christ? Is Jesus truly the God of *Heaven's Gates, Hell's Flames*, wielding eternity like a threat? Is He a peace-loving hippie who's cool with whatever we choose? Or is He something else entirely?

ENDING THE DEVIL'S ENTERPRISE

"The reason the Son of God appeared was to destroy the works of the devil" (1 John 3:8).

Works in this verse refers to a "business or enterprise and all its achievements."[71] The incarnation was heaven's declaration to permanently dismantle the enemy's operation. Jesus came as the promised seed of Genesis 3, the One who would crush the serpent's head at great cost to Himself (Genesis 3:15).

Jesus came to decimate every evil stronghold against God (2 Corinthians 10:5). He demolished every brick the accuser cemented to obscure our view of the Father. Jesus removed every last slur of graffiti that vandalized the image of God imprinted on our hearts. Our King did this by removing the walls that divided us. He tore down both the veil that kept us from God and the barriers we had built to keep each other out.

The gates of hell, once seen as impenetrable fortresses of ownership, would melt in His wake, rendered useless forever.

But that raises the million-dollar question. How did Jesus accomplish this?

EMPTYING HELL'S CLAIM BY EMPTYING HIMSELF

In his letter to the Philippians, Paul wrote that Jesus "emptied himself…being born in the likeness of men" (Philippians 2:7). The Greek word for *empty* is *kenosis*. I can't hear it today without remembering the heated dorm debates from my Bible college days—discussions dissecting which divine attributes Jesus set aside during His time on Earth. But in all the theological sparring, we often missed the most obvious and breathtaking truth. God's response to our emptiness was not wrath or vengeance. It was to empty Himself.

"When you were dead in your sins…God made you alive with Christ. He forgave us all our sins, having canceled the charge…he has taken it away, nailing it to the cross. And having disarmed the powers and authorities, he made a public spectacle of them, triumphing over them by the cross" (Colossians 2:13–15 NIV).

How did Jesus disarm the enemy and make a spectacle of him, hanging him by his underwear on the proverbial flagpole, stripped of all rights and power? He forgave.

Jesus didn't flood heaven by filling us with threats of hell. He instead emptied any claim the darkness could hope to hold over humanity by emptying Himself.

He traded our violence for His vulnerability. Our emptiness for His fullness.

He is never found wielding the tools of Satan to cast out Satan, because we will never establish lasting peace through violence.

This is the scandal of the gospel.

Jesus makes us *live* by choosing to *die*.

He brings us *light* by walking straight into the *darkness*.

He *fills* us by *pouring Himself out*.

This is how hell loses its grip. Still, some recoil passionately, "Sure, Jesus was loving, but He was angry, too!"

"He flipped tables! Cursed fig trees! Talked more about hell than anything else!"

"He came first on a cross, but He's coming back with a sword!"

I hear this posture far too often, a strange satisfaction in imagining Jesus finally dishing out divine payback. But as I unpack further in my book *En(d)titlement*, Jesus' anger in the temple and His symbolic act with the fig tree weren't the responses of an unhinged man. He wasn't throwing a fit. He was casting down systems of pride and violence that masqueraded as holiness for too long.

As we step into some difficult questions about hell, wrath, and the book of Revelation, we must hold fast to two anchor points.

First, God is majestic.

He is Creator, Sustainer, and King. He governs wonders we cannot begin to grasp and beauty that takes our breath away. His ways are not like ours (Isaiah 55:9). They're better. We will not presume to think that because something does not make sense to us, it cannot be holy and altogether true. God has made His goodness unmistakable. He is not on trial.

Second, God is mysterious.

In His grace, God has drawn near, and yet there are still many places we still can't see or understand Him clearly (1 Corinthians 13:12). Aspects of God's story will defy our comprehension. That's just part of being human and walking by faith.

In the pages ahead, we will not find answers to every question. Nor will I make any effort to sanitize or redefine the story into theologies more palatable to our sensibilities. Why? Because I genuinely believe God is good. He doesn't need to be rescued from His Word. But we do need to learn to slow down, read in context, and carry a willingness to let tired assumptions die.

We won't come trembling in fear of judgment.

We don't come burning with a desire for vengeance.

We carry only one desire as Paul prayed in Ephesians 3:19, "To know the love of Christ that surpasses knowledge, that you may be filled with all the fullness of God."

May we see the love of God clearly, especially when He leads us through the refiner's fire.

HELL

"Jesus taught more about hell than anyone." It's a common claim. But is it true?

Well, that depends on what you mean by *hell.*

Most modern readers are unaware that our English Bibles translate three distinct words—Gehenna, Hades, and Tartarus—into the single word *hell,* although each carries a significantly different meaning. While some of the words echo traditional ideas of postmortem judgment, others point to something else entirely.

And when we take time to discover what Jesus said about hell, and who He was talking to, what emerges is far more compelling, challenging, and beautiful than the version of the gospel many of us inherited, one more focused on escaping hell than embodying heaven. Let's unpack these words in their original context.

Gehenna "The Valley of Hinnom"[72]

Of all the New Testament words translated as hell, none appears more frequently than Gehenna, a Greek transliteration of *Gē-Hinnom,* meaning "The Valley of Hinnom." This was not an abstract underworld but a ravine outside the walls of Jerusalem. And for Israel, it carried a long, shameful memory.

Some of Israel's darkest sins unfolded in this valley. Under the reigns of Kings Ahaz and Manasseh, God's people committed unthinkable acts, sacrificing their own children in fire to the false gods Molech and Baal. To secure blessing, they hurled their sons and daughters into flames, believing their suffering somehow pleased the gods.[73] Later, King Josiah desecrated and destroyed the site, ending the carnage.

Over time, tradition holds that Gehenna became Jerusalem's refuse heap filled with burning trash, dead animals, and the bodies of criminals too disgraced for burial.[74] By Jesus' day, Gehenna was a symbol of sin, ruin, waste, and irreversible loss. It was a vivid warning, a place where God's people once traded their calling for idolatry, their inheritance for fire.

Jesus referred to Gehenna eleven times, in three specific contexts. We'll look briefly at each and discover what He was warning us about.

Context 1: Cut it off

Of the eleven times Jesus referenced Gehenna, seven appear in one recurring theme. They're not spoken to pagans, skeptics, or rebellious crowds. Jesus spoke these words to His own disciples.

Let that sink in.

Jesus' fiercest words about hell weren't warnings for the lost. They were for us. He wasn't preaching fear to outsiders but confronting compromise *inside* the family of God. Gehenna wasn't an external destination God threatened to send people—it was an internal desire Jesus instructed His followers to root out of their lives.

This urgency appears in three lessons, recorded twice for emphasis, once in the Sermon on the Mount and later while teaching His disciples.

1. Lesson on murder: "and whoever says, 'You fool!' will be liable to the hell [Gehenna] of fire" (Matthew 5:22).
2. Lesson on lust: "If your right eye causes you to sin, tear it out and throw it away. For, it is better that you lose one of your members than that your whole body be thrown into hell [Gehenna]" (Matthew 5:29).
3. Lesson on leading the vulnerable astray: "If your hand or your foot causes you to sin, cut it off and throw it away. It is better for you to enter life crippled or lame than with two hands or two feet to be thrown into the eternal fire [Gehenna]" (Matthew 18:8).

These aren't three different ideas. They are three expressions of one deeper call to cut off anything in your heart that leads to death. Let's consider the first. "You have heard that it was said to the people long ago, 'You shall not murder...But I tell you that...anyone who says, 'You fool!' will be in danger of the fire of hell [Gehenna]" (Matthew 5:21–22 NIV).

We briefly addressed Jesus' teaching on murder in chapter 8, but it is worth returning to for the discussion here. Note the progression. Someone angry with their brother or sister is *warned of judgment* (a trial). Next, one who goes beyond anger to shout, "Raca," an ancient slur that demeaned someone as worthless, could *face the Sanhedrin*, their religious court. Finally, one who deems in their heart their brother a fool (the ancient word meaning empty or an idiot) stands i*n danger of Gehenna.*

This prompts several questions. Was God, the same God who promised in John 10:29 NIV, "No one can snatch them out of my Father's hand," now levying a standard higher than the impossible Mosaic Law? Was He threatening eternal torment if our performance falters?

The answers are yes and no. Yes, because throughout the Sermon on the Mount, Jesus was unquestionably intensifying the Law—not relaxing it but raising it to its fullest meaning. He didn't lower the bar; He lifted it beyond external obedience to expose and transform the very motives of our hearts, revealing our need for a Savior.

The Law commanded the Israelites not to murder. Jesus called us to surrender every thought, word, or supposed right to devalue another human being, the root of all murder.

But no. Jesus doesn't lay a burden on us to perform in our own strength or else. Do we really think calling someone a fool places us on the precipice of burning in anguish forever? If so, a whole lot of drivers in rush hour traffic are in grave danger. They *think* they're headed home, but they are on the highway to hell! *We know better.*

Jesus was teaching that this attitude has no place in His kingdom. It does not reflect the new heart and Spirit He put within us. Wherever we see these attitudes at work in us, we need to *cut them off*, sending them to the garbage heap. Otherwise, we're doing the same thing the worshippers of Molech and Baal did, sacrificing precious kids in the valley to satisfy the agenda of a false god.

Scholars note the use of hyperbole, or intentional exaggeration, to drive a point home. For example, when Jesus said that anyone who struggled with lust should gouge out their eyes or cut off their hands, He wasn't calling for self-mutilation. He was begging us to see that these *postures* have no part in who we have become in Christ. Our old nature was cut off, and now we're invited to imprison every single dispute against God (2 Corinthians 10:4–5). At His throne of grace, we can surrender these unholy, prideful, violent attitudes into the refiner's fire, where He burns away the dross of everything that isn't ours anymore.

Context 2: "Do Not Fear...Fear...Do Not Fear"

Jesus' second mention of Gehenna surfaced in a jarring moment when he said, "Do not fear those who kill the body but cannot kill the soul. Rather fear him who can destroy both soul and body in hell [Gehenna]" (Matthew 10:28).

At face value, this sounds like an ominous warning to the disciples. They should cower in fear before a God who might obliterate them in hell. However, this interpretation quickly collapses when we read the passage in context.

This was no fire-and-brimstone sermon aimed at outsiders. This was Jesus, commissioning His disciples for ministry. It's their *ordination speech*. And it's filled with repeated reassurances to them.

"*Do not be afraid* of them [those who would persecute you], for there is nothing concealed that will not be disclosed, or hidden that will not be made known...*Do not be afraid* of those who kill the body but cannot kill the soul. Rather, *be afraid* of the One who can destroy both soul and body in hell [Gehenna]. Are not two sparrows sold for a penny? Yet not one of them will fall to the ground outside your Father's care. And even the very hairs of your head are all numbered. *So don't be afraid*; you are worth more than many sparrows" (Matthew 10:26–31 NIV, emphasis mine).

As Jesus sent them into uncharted waters, He desired to *remove* fear. This is the motivation behind His words.

Jesus wasn't playing good-cop, bad-cop with the disciples' fragile emotions to keep them under His thumb. He wasn't trying to frighten them, but to *free* them. By naming every fear swirling in their minds—rejection, suffering, even death. He promised, "You don't need to be afraid of the world out there. Only fear One. And know that He's counted every strand of hair on your head and anointed you for the task ahead, so don't be afraid."

At the same time, with Judas standing in their midst, His words also carried a warning about the gravity of using God's name to advance our own kingdom, instead of standing in awe of the One to whom we will ultimately give an account.

Context 3: A Rebuke and Warning

Until now, Jesus' words about Gehenna were directed to His disciples, a call to examine their own hearts and cut off anything that doesn't belong in their kingdom identity. But in Matthew 23, Jesus' focus and tone shifted dramatically. Here, He turned to the religious leaders with a fiery rebuke and an unflinching warning.

"Woe to you, scribes and Pharisees, hypocrites! For you travel across sea and land to make a single proselyte, and when he becomes a proselyte, you make him twice as much a child of hell [Gehenna] as yourselves...You serpents, you brood of vipers, how are you to escape being sentenced to hell [Gehenna]?" (Matthew 23:15, 33).

This sobering declaration falls within what is often called the Seven Woes, a final indictment of religious leaders who weaponized the Law to exalt themselves and crush others. Seven, the number of completeness, signals the totality of their corruption. In one of His last public messages to them, Jesus exposed the full depth of their spiritual distortion.

First, He confronted them as *children of Gehenna*, mirroring the same horrors their ancestors committed in that fated valley. Yet, they were guilty of worse. The former caused the destruction of bodies, but they sacrificed souls in the fires of their religion.

Second, Jesus issued a sobering question. It literally read, "What can be done to stop you from *separating yourselves* permanently into the judgment of Gehenna?"[75]

It wasn't a declaration of doom. It was a desperate plea. Just as the days of Noah when humanity was destroying themselves, Jesus begged those who spent their lives studying His Word to open their eyes and see Him.

Jesus was not pronouncing final judgment; He was holding the door open for repentance. And He still is. The warning was severe because the consequences of their pride were catastrophic. But even here, the invitation remained. Turn around. *Come home.*

Hades the Grave; the Realm of the Dead[76]

The New Testament uses the word *Hades* eleven times, closely mirroring the Old Testament's *Sheol*, often translated as "the grave" or "the realm of the dead."[77] While English Bibles often merge these words under the catch-all label *hell*, Hades carries a range of meanings deserving deeper exploration. In the New Testament, it appears in three distinct contexts.

Context 1: A simple reference to death

In Acts 2, Peter quoted Psalm 16 to proclaim the Father did not abandon Jesus to the realm of the dead.

"I saw the Lord always before me, for he is at my right hand that I may not be shaken; therefore my heart was glad, and my tongue rejoiced; my flesh also will dwell in hope. For you will not abandon my soul to Hades, or let your Holy One see corruption" (Acts 2:25–27).

The Hebrew word *Sheol* becomes Hades in Greek, signaling not eternal torment, but death itself. In fact, most modern translations render all sixty-six Old Testament uses of Sheol as the grave or death, with no usage equal to what we traditionally call hell.[78] In this sense, Hades simply means death.

Context 2: The power structure of the kingdom of darkness

At other times, Hades refers to the operating system of Satan's rule—an oppressive kingdom that Jesus came to dismantle. Jesus declared to His disciples, "I will build my church, and the gates of hell

[Hades] shall not prevail against it" (Matthew 16:18).

Gates symbolize authority and control, marking the boundaries of what a kingdom claims as its own. Jesus promised the fortified walls of darkness would not hold against His advancing kingdom. In Revelation 1:18, Jesus is holding "the keys of Death and Hades." Keys denote authority. They lock and they unlock. Whatever locked us out of life, and whatever confined us in fear, has now been unlocked by the cross.

In a staggering act of trust, Jesus gave His church the keys of the kingdom—empowering her to unlock heaven's purposes and restrain whatever hinders God's reign on earth (Matthew 16:19). Hades is a kingdom in collapse. And Jesus is the wrecking ball.

Context 3: A place of future judgment

While the word *Hades* carries multiple layers of meaning, its use in a few key passages takes on a sobering tone—depicting a future judgment for those who persistently reject the way of life. One of Jesus' most startling warnings came not to pagans or oppressors but to the town of Capernaum. He warned, "And you, Capernaum, will you be lifted to the heavens? No, you will go down to Hades. For if the miracles that were performed in you had been performed in Sodom, it would have remained to this day" (Matthew 11:23–24 NIV).

His rebuke shocked those listening because Capernaum wasn't a random village. It had been His base of operations, Jesus' hometown. In Capernaum, Jesus called the first disciples. He healed a centurion's servant and a nobleman's son. Peter's mother-in-law was raised from her sick bed, and a paralytic walked again. In this town He raised Jairus' daughter from the dead and cast out unclean spirits. He also offered Himself as the Bread of Life (John 6:25–29).

This town witnessed all these wonders yet refused to repent.

Jesus' words serve as a warning. We will be held accountable for the revelation we've received. That said, it's important to recognize that while the warning was a heartfelt plea for individuals to turn to Him, it was addressed not to individuals, but to the city as a whole. This was certainly not a warning for every citizen who resided in the zip code, as many of them were faithful followers of Jesus. This was a warning for the *city's legacy* in the halls of history. The *way of Capernaum* would not be able to enter the kingdom, and its refusal to change would lead to its collapse.

Hades is mentioned one final time at the close of Scripture, in a vision of the final judgment.

"The sea gave up the dead that were in it, and death and Hades gave up the dead that were in them…Then death and Hades were thrown into the lake of fire. The lake of fire is the second death. Anyone whose name was not found written in the book of life was thrown into the lake of fire" (Revelation 20:13–15).

In this Scripture, Hades is personified and judged—not as a location alone, but as *the spiritual system that unleashed death across the earth*. God never intended this destruction for people but for the devil and his angels (Matthew 25:41). And yet, the tragic conclusion in Revelation 20 reveals some will still cling to the way of death and Hades with a white-knuckled grip. Even as their violent empires crumble, they will not let go.

I wish parts of this story weren't true. But we do no one a favor by softening the pieces that break our hearts. Truth doesn't crush us—it frees us. And even *this* truth, spoken in the light of the Father's face, can become an invitation for many to come home. "You will know the truth, and the truth will set you free" (John 8:32).

So, we speak with compassion. We warn with humility. And we keep hoping, not in fear, but in radiant faith that the light still shines, and the Father still waits for His kids to come home.

Tartarus: "The abyss"[79]

The final Greek word translated as *hell* appears only once in the New Testament.

"God did not spare angels when they sinned, but cast them into hell [Tartarus] and committed them to chains of gloomy darkness to be kept until the judgment…then the Lord knows how to rescue the godly from trials, and to keep the unrighteous under punishment until the day of judgment" (2 Peter 2:4, 9).

In ancient Greek and Roman mythology, Tartarus was a deep abyss where the enemies of the gods were cast into chains. Just as Gehenna evoked vivid associations for Jewish audiences familiar with its historical and prophetic weight, Tartarus would have struck a powerful chord with Gentiles steeped in their own cultural myths. In its sole appearance in Scripture, Tartarus is a place where fallen angels are held while they await the day of judgment.

Peter wrote to strengthen and encourage believers facing exploitation and suffering at the hands of false teachers.

As God always has, He will remain faithful. He rescues the godly from trials and deals justly with those who reject His way.

This passage also served as a sobering warning about a coming day of judgment to anyone who used power to exploit, defile, or mislead the vulnerable (2 Peter 2:10). Yet, even in the midst of this warning, God's mercy reigns. While fallen angels have been cast into Tartarus while they await judgment, the unrighteous are afforded a different grace. Peter declared that God saves the devout from testing and keeps the sinful under *punishment*, a word meaning "to prune, correct, or restrain."[80] Even now, our great God holds evil in check while zealously pursuing those caught in it with the kindness that leads us back to Him (Romans 2:4). Our God is the long road of mercy and the unwavering champion of justice.

A CONCLUSION ON HELL

So, where does all this leave us?

First, let's resist two extremes when it comes to judgment—obsession on one hand, and avoidance on the other.

Moving Beyond Obsession

I understand the passion driving some believers to urgently warn others of sin's consequences. I share that same ache for the world to know God's love. But I must also express genuine concern about how many Christians attempt to deliver this message, often in ways that distort the very heart of the gospel.

First, we tend to confuse *proclamation* with *incarnation*. Shouting at strangers is not the same as embodying the gospel in our neighborhoods. Jesus didn't show up with a picket sign and a megaphone. He moved in. He broke bread. He wept. He healed. He stayed. And He warned, but always in the context of relational love.

Second, the people we think need to be warned the most concerning hell don't match the people Jesus warned. Every culture elevates one or two sins as *the* thing destroying their culture, while turning a blind eye to many other grave injustices. For first-century Jews, it was tax collectors and sinners. We have our own version of these today. Here's my concern. Jesus warned *religious people*, but He did everything possible to draw near to wayward *prodigal orphans*, so they could experience the love of the Father. We often do precisely the opposite.

When our gospel begins with fear, it can easily distort the Father's heart. This greatly concerns me. We end up offering people fire insurance rather than transformation.

But what could happen if we start from the truth of the Father's adoration for them instead? What if they understand the message of God's love because they see it in what they receive from us? It would be a more beautiful, more truthful gospel.

Moving Beyond Avoidance

On the other side, many today swing the pendulum toward silence, as they sweep judgment out of the story entirely under the vague banner of *God is love*. But love isn't indifferent. It is holy.

The Jesus of the tolerance movement who simply applauds as we each speak our own truth, is not the gospel. There is no *my truth*. There's only truth. Truth is a Person and His name is Jesus. And that's great news, because Jesus didn't come to merely tolerate us. He came to transform us.

Love tells the truth. It never stands in silent complicity with the things that destroy us. Sin kills us. It always has. But Jesus came so *all* could turn from death and live.

So...how are we to think about hell now? Consider the words of C.S. Lewis. "I willingly believe that the damned are, in one sense, successful, rebels to the end; that the doors of hell are locked on the inside. I do not mean that the ghosts may not wish to come out of hell, in the vague fashion wherein one man 'wishes' to be happy: but they certainly do not will even the first preliminary stages of that self-abandonment through which alone the soul can reach any good. They enjoy forever the horrible freedom they have demanded, and are therefore self-enslaved: just as the blessed, forever submitting to obedience, become through all eternity more and more free."[81]

The doors of hell are locked *on the inside*.

Jesus' parable of the rich man and Lazarus in Luke 16 paints this truth. The rich man lived a life of comfort disregarding those in need. He feasted while Lazarus suffered at his gate. In death, their fortunes are reversed. But notice, even in torment the rich man never repented. From Hades, he still wished to command Lazarus like a servant. He wanted relief, yes, but not transformation. In the end, Lazarus stood free, known for all eternity as the beloved child he'd always been...and the rich man faded into oblivion with neither face nor name.

Hell, in this light, is not so much a sentence imposed on us but a disposition selected by us. It is the tragic end of a life built around pride, privilege, and self-worship. A life that refuses the way of love.

Heaven and hell aren't only about where we go when we die. They're about the kingdom we're choosing to live from, right now and forever.

We don't need to weaponize hell to scare people into heaven. Nor do we need to tone down Jesus to try to make Him more appealing to modern tastes. The gospel is already beautiful enough.

Knowing this, we can passionately invite the world to receive the life that is truly life. Not because they're scared, but because they're loved.

DISCUSSION QUESTIONS

1. How have fear-based presentations of the gospel, like *Heaven's Gates, Hell's Flames*, shaped your faith, either positively or negatively? Explain.
2. How does reexamining the biblical language around hell, Gehenna, Hades, and Tartarus, challenge or confirm what you previously believed about God's judgment and justice?
3. What if the goal is to show them the beauty and wholeness of the life we can have in Christ? How might your view of evangelism shift if the goal isn't to scare people out of hell and into heaven?

TEN

TERMINATOR JESUS?

Disarming the violence we project onto the Prince of Peace

IT WAS THE SUMMER OF 1741, during a season of intense religious revival in America known as the First Great Awakening. In a quiet church in Enfield, Connecticut, a visiting preacher named Jonathan Edwards stepped behind the pulpit with a message that would leave a permanent mark—not only on the trembling congregation before him, but on the shape of American theology for centuries to come.

The sermon, titled "Sinners in the Hands of an Angry God," anchored on a single Old Testament verse, "It is mine to avenge; I will repay. In due time their foot will slip; their day of disaster is near and their doom rushes upon them" (Deuteronomy 32:35, NIV).

Edwards' delivery was said to be nearly monotone, read from a manuscript without dramatic flourish. And yet, he conjured images that ignited fear into the hearts of all who listened and many who have read it since. Consider just a few direct lines from the sermon.

- "The bow of God's wrath is bent, and the arrow made ready on the string…the pit is prepared, the fire is ready, the furnace is hot, the flames do rage and glow."
- "The God that holds you over the pit of hell, much as one holds a spider or some loathsome insect over the fire, abhors you…

You are ten thousand times more abominable in his eyes than the most hateful venomous serpent is in ours."

- "He will have no compassion upon you…there shall be no moderation or mercy…no regard to your welfare…No place shall be thought fit for you but under his feet to be trodden down as the mire of the streets."

Edwards closed with an urgent plea, "The wrath of Almighty God is now undoubtedly hanging over a great part of this congregation. Let everyone fly out of Sodom: 'Haste and escape for your lives, look not behind you, escape to the mountain, lest you be consumed.'"[82]

The response was electric. Eyewitnesses described moaning and wailing erupting throughout the sanctuary. Some clung white-knuckled to their pews, convinced they were mere moments from falling into the flames of hell. Others collapsed to the floor, begging for mercy, sobbing, shaking, unable to hear the sermon's conclusion over the sound of their own despair.[83]

The people were shaken. Moved. Frightened into a form of repentance. And ever since, "Sinners in the Hands of an Angry God" has been hailed by many as the most important sermon in American history.[84]

Let that sink in.

This fear-drenched image of God has shaped far more than one moment in church history. It has profoundly influenced how we present the gospel, and more than that, how we see God. For many, it forged a framework of fear-based evangelism, guilt-driven spirituality, and a picture of divine justice that looks more like mob vengeance than cruciform love.

If God's wrath seems at odds with His love, what do we do with that tension?

We have to step out of the fog of fear and inherited assumptions and return to the one place where His heart is seen without distortion—the cross. It's here that love and justice meet, and through this lens, God invites us to see everything else.

WRATH

In the Hebrew Scriptures, wrath is not a single concept but a family of images of flared nostrils, burning heat, overflowing waters, even foaming rage. Together, these appear nearly four hundred times, yet they describe something far deeper than divine temper. They reveal God's protective love and His passionate opposition to everything that threatens or destroys His beloved.

It's no minor theme in the story, and its raw language can shake us. What are we to make of it? Is God tender-hearted toward humanity or furious? To see God's wrath clearly, we'll need to anchor ourselves in three foundational truths that reveal what wrath really is in the light of the cross.

The first foundational truth reminds us God's anger is not like ours.

There is a world of difference between being angry about something and letting that anger lead you into sin. Paul told the Ephesians, "In your anger do not sin" (Ephesians 4:26 NIV). Anger, biblically defined, is a deep stirring of the soul in response to something broken, particularly when it affects someone you love. It's a refusal to be passive in the face of injustice.

God hates sin because sin destroys what He loves.

We rarely keep anger and sin apart, and that's the problem. When we face injustice, our anger often gets tangled with fear. Before long, that fear-driven fury lashes out. We shout, manipulate, control, and wound. But God never reacts from fear, never loses control, never stoops to pettiness or insecurity. His anger is love in motion. A protective passion that rises not to crush, but to restore. And in the end, it's His kindness, not His fury, that leads us home in repentance (Romans 2:4).

The second truth we must stand on is that God's anger is not a protest against us. It's the pursuit of us.

Scripture tells us God is jealous for us, describing His love as a consuming fire (Deuteronomy 4:24). That image once bothered me. It sounded too much like the controlling, insecure love I've seen between broken people. But God's jealousy is nothing like ours. He isn't jealous to get something from us but to give something to us.

This is not the temperamental, toxic love we know from human experience. It is the ache of passion that keeps reaching for us even when rejected. God's anger burns, but not to destroy. He is the refiner's fire drawing near to consume everything that steals from us, poisons us, or masquerades as love.

Many theologians, from the early church fathers to today, have wondered if, in the end, there is only one fire of God. One flame of divine love that comes to purify whatever it touches. For the heart yielded to Him, that fire feels like heaven in all of its brilliance. But for the one clinging to pride, violence, or vengeance, the same fire feels like hell, because it threatens the very death they've come to call life.

In this sense, the anger of God is the tension between His gift of free will and His utter unwillingness to abandon us to the ruin we've chosen. His anger is love's determination to destroy whatever destroys us and the patient pursuit of our hearts to encounter the One we were made for.

A picture might help. I adore my wife, Jill. She is my best friend. We met when she was fourteen and I was fifteen, and I'm pretty sure I loved her instantly. She has all my heart, and I cannot imagine any world without Jill in it. So, imagine my waking tomorrow to a reality where Jill no longer remembered me. If I saw her mistreated by someone who refused to treasure her, I couldn't stay passive. My heart would turn within me to do whatever it takes to bring her back to safety. Because I love her.

This is how God feels about you.

You are His beloved.

When false lovers make promises that steal your gaze and break your heart, God is not indifferent. When the world toys with your worth, He is stirred—not against you, but for you. Even now, His consuming fire draws near to heal and refine, burning away shame and fear, to the degree you let Him. And unlike us, God never spirals into cruelty or coercion. He gently and relentlessly pursues.

The third foundational truth is that the language of wrath is *for us*.

When my kids were little, there were plenty of moments when Jill and I brought gentle guidance, patient reminders, and loving redirection to attitudes that were out of bounds. But sometimes, despite every warning, we'd see them spiraling. An angry shove, a cutting word, a defiant act that demanded immediate correction. In those moments, we had to raise our voices to get their attention. They weren't ready for nuance. They needed urgency. I spoke with a firm tone, a furrowed brow, and sometimes a necessary consequence. But as soon as I left the room, I often glanced at Jill with a smile, because I wasn't unhinged. I was simply doing what was needed for them to grow. (For the record, my own frustration leaked through plenty of times, but that's another story).

I'm convinced God is a far better parent than I am. Much of what we read as divine wrath in Scripture, especially in Israel's childhood wanderings and seasons of exile, is God coming low to His wayward kids, speaking in a tone they'd understand. I'm not minimizing the severity of God's warnings or the grave danger of giving ourselves over to sin. I am simply inviting us to see these moments in clearer context through the lens of the Father who looks like Jesus.

The Bible goes to great lengths to show that God exists outside of time, and His redemptive work was already complete before creation itself.

- "The Lamb who was slain from the creation of the world" (Revelation 13:8 NIV).
- "He was chosen before the creation of the world, but was revealed in these last times for your sake" (1 Peter 1:20 NIV).
- "Blessed be the God and Father of our Lord Jesus Christ, who… chose us in him before the foundation of the world, that we should be holy and blameless before him" (Ephesians 1:3–4).
- "His works were finished from the foundation of the world" (Hebrews 4:3).
- "God…who saved us and called us to a holy calling, not because of our works but because of his own purpose and grace, which he gave us in Christ Jesus before the ages began, and which now has been manifested through the appearing of our Savior Christ Jesus, who abolished death" (2 Timothy 1:8–10).

Somehow, before humanity ever drew its first breath, God had already given His last to redeem us. He knew our choices, our violence, our pride, and He bore the cost of all of it before the story even began. Whatever we imagine *the wrath of God* to mean, we must understand that God had already carried it upon His own shoulders before He ever spoke of it to humanity.

Before the Garden, God was already somewhere hanging on the cross.

And when the moment came for history to unfold, as Peter penned, it was all for our sake. It's baffling and beautiful.

As a child, I was taught that God was so angry at my sin He couldn't bear to even look at me. That He killed His Son instead and now looks past my wretchedness only to see Jesus' transactional purchase. That view deals with the severity of sin, but at what cost?

Jesus is the full revelation of who the Father has always been. We do the majesty of God great injustice when we divide Him into some cosmic good-cop/bad-cop split personality. The cross wasn't the Father's violent reaction to our sin. It was the Trinity's united response to rescue us from sin. God Himself, all of Him—Father, Son, and Spirit—loved us so much He took upon Himself the violence we unleashed, carrying it away once and for all.

We sinned. All of us. And our sin reaped its own destruction. Our wrath gave every reason for God to pour His wrath upon us. But instead, He placed it all upon Himself.

"He was pierced for our transgressions, he was crushed for our iniquities; the punishment that brought us peace was on him, and by his wounds we are healed" (Isaiah 53:5 NIV).

The cross didn't come to end God's anger.

It came to end ours.

So, what do we do with passages of Scripture that speak of God's wrath? How do we read them through the lens of the cross? Many of these passages appear in the prophets and are often misunderstood, largely because we stop reading too soon. But when we keep going, we see a recurring pattern.

God's anger always gives way to tenderness.

His justice always bends toward mercy.

Just as quickly as He declares judgment, He softens into the voice of a broken-hearted Father.

"How can I give you up, Ephraim? How can I hand you over, Israel?...My heart is changed within me; all my compassion is aroused. I will not carry out my fierce anger...For I am God, and not a man" (Hosea 11:8–9 NIV).

God's "anger lasts only a moment, but his favor lasts a lifetime" (Psalm 30:5 NIV).

And yet even knowing He's finished His work and His love has triumphed, Scripture reminds us our choices still carry great weight. Love never forces itself. As I shared earlier in the discussion on hell, God has given humanity the dignity of a real will. We can, it seems, cling to our allegiance to violence and pride and reject the One who came to heal us.

This is part of the reason the Bible's language about wrath carries such urgency. It's not the raging of an unhinged deity. It's the pleading voice of a Father who has gone to every length to save His children yet will not force their love.

As John wrote: "For God did not send his Son into the world to condemn the world, but to save the world through him. Whoever believes in him is not condemned, but whoever does not believe stands condemned already because they have not believed in the name of God's one and only Son. This is the verdict: Light has come into the world, but people loved darkness instead of light" (John 3:17–19 NIV).

And again, "Whoever believes in the Son has eternal life; whoever does not obey the Son shall not see life, but the wrath of God remains on him" (John 3:36).

This isn't the fury of a vengeful god, but the heartbreak of divine love watching its children choose ruin over restoration. It's the cry of mercy itself, pleading for us to come home.

And here's the sobering truth. Jesus' strongest warnings were never aimed at the wounded, the wandering, or the weak. They were spoken to those who dared to stand in the high place of self-righteousness, while looking down on others still reaching for grace. His words were, and still are, a plea to awaken the self-assured and to remind every heart that only grace saves.

For as He said, "Many who are first will be last, and the last first" (Matthew 19:30).

Selah.

JESUS OR THE TERMINATOR

On more than one occasion, I've been met with offense, sometimes even anger, over my teaching that Jesus is the full revelation of the Father. The response is usually the same. Red-faced resistance, coupled with a puffed-up bravado informing me that Jesus isn't just some love-your-enemies, peace-making softie. Then, with something bordering on patriotic pride, they paint their favorite picture.

Jesus on a war horse. Veins bulging. Tattooed.

His robe drenched in blood, sword drawn, ready to annihilate the wicked and finally clean house. This, they tell me, is *their* Jesus. The divine version of *my God could beat up your God.*

Father, forgive us.

Is this really the Jesus of the book of Revelation? A cosmic executioner, dripping with vengeance, ready to make heads roll? Terminator Jesus? (I mean, they do share the same catchphrase, *I'll be back*, but still.)

Are we really to believe at His return, Jesus will abandon the nonviolent kingdom He announced in the Sermon on the Mount?

What are we missing in plain sight?

We would do well to remember the Bible's final book isn't a rebrand of Jesus. It is the *revelation* of Jesus. The same Lamb who conquered by laying down His life is the One unveiled in glory, not as a retreat from Calvary, but as its radiant fulfillment.

Let's look together at four keys to what God is truly doing as He comes on the clouds.

Key 1: The Purpose of the Book of Revelation

As a pastor of twenty-five years, I am surprised by how many faithful Jesus-followers quietly admit they don't like the book of Revelation. For many, it's a confusing mix of doom, judgment, and bizarre symbolism. Some see it as an end times checklist to make sure we don't accidentally take the Mark of the Beast. Others see it as an almanac for fringe prophecy buffs to predict future disasters.

But that's not the story of Revelation. Pay attention to how John opens the book.

"The revelation of Jesus Christ, which God gave him to show to his servants the things that must soon take place...Blessed is the one who reads aloud the words of this prophecy, and blessed are those who hear, and who keep what is written in it, for the time is near" (Revelation 1:1a, 3).

Revelation is not a coded horror story or a rapture roadmap. It is the coronation of the Lamb.

And according to John, the result of reading it right is blessing. Not fear. The Greek word translated *blessed* here literally means *to be deliriously happy*![85] In other words, if you're reading Revelation and you aren't exploding with joy, you're reading it wrong.

That's our first clue. For followers of Jesus, Revelation isn't a book of dread. It's a declaration of delight.

Key 2: A book full of symbols

Revelation is apocalyptic literature, vivid, poetic, and saturated with symbols that point beyond themselves to deeper truths. If we miss this, we'll end up in strange, and often harmful, theological territory. From the very first chapter, it is clear. Revelation isn't meant to be read like the Gospel of Matthew. This isn't a documentary. It's a divine tapestry woven with symbols from across the whole biblical story.

For those who know their Bibles, it's like uncovering sacred Easter eggs—only way better than Pixar. John's vision is bursting with imagery.

- Lampstands that are churches. (Revelation 1:20)
- Stars that are angels. (Revelation 1:20)
- Creatures with faces, eyes, and wings that are majestic servants.

(Revelation 4:6–8)

- Incense bowls that are the prayers of the saints. (Revelation 5:8)
- Horses who represent coming actions on the earth. (Revelation 6)
- 144,000 "sealed ones" who represent the fullness of redemption, 12,000 of each of the twelve tribes. (Revelation 7)
- Trumpets that are tribulations. (Revelation 8)
- Locusts that represent coming trials. (Revelation 9)

And the symbols get wilder still. A mighty angel straddling two continents, a pregnant woman clothed with the sun, and a dragon sweeping stars out of heaven, a *beast* with crowns and blasphemous names, another *beast* who looks like a lamb but speaks like a dragon, a great prostitute seated on many waters (Revelation 10, 12, 13, and 17).

This is not literal anatomy or cosmic horror. It's prophetic poetry on an epic scale.

The churches aren't literal lampstands. The angels aren't literal stars. The worshipping beings don't literally have four faces with eyes all around. (That's terrifying.)

This is a grand scale poetic parade of *symbols*, each intentionally communicated to reveal our coming life after death. We must not read Revelation forcing a strict literalism that denies what the images represent. I take great issue with people turning the unveiling of our King into a horror story loaded with jump scares. It paints an image unworthy of the gospel. Brian Zahnd wisely warns, "When we literalize the militant images of Revelation we arrive at this conclusion: in the end even Jesus gives up on love and resorts to violence. Tragically, those who refuse to embrace the way of peace taught by Jesus use the symbolic war of Revelation 19 to silence the Sermon on the Mount. This kind of hermeneutic has disastrous implications."[86]

Revelation isn't a puzzle to solve. It's a Prince to behold.

Key 3: The Savior on a white horse

"Then I saw heaven opened, and behold, a white horse! The one sitting on it is called Faithful and True, and in righteousness he judges and makes war" (Revelation 19:11).

The animal a king rides reveals the nature of the kingdom he brings.

Jesus came at His triumphal entry on a beast of burden *because He came to carry ours*. That has never changed. But here, in Revelation 19, we see a new dimension of His reign. This time, Jesus appears riding a white horse. Elsewhere in Revelation, we encounter a horse of war (red), a horse of famine (black), and a horse of death (pale). But Jesus did not sit upon any of them. Why? Because the animal a king sits on reveals the kingdom he sets upon you.

We've had our fill of the death horses. So, our King appears on a pure white horse. And the One who rides it? His name is Faithful and True. Do you remember the words Jesus promised we'd long to hear when He comes back for us? He said, "Well done, good and faithful servant" (Matthew 25:21 NIV).

He rode as the One called Faithful because He'd come to make us faithful.

How about this one? Jesus promised, "And you will know the truth and the truth will set you free" (John 8:32). He rode as the One called True because the Truth had come at last to fully and finally set us free.

He rides into history's final battle not to conquer using death, but to restore *righteousness*, returning creation to the way it was always meant to be.[87] Look back at Revelation 19:11, "and in righteousness, he judges and makes war." This war is none other than the climax He foretold in Genesis 3. Creation was finally going back to Eden, just as He promised.

The story continues. Jesus' eyes are like a flame of fire, because He is the Light of the World. His robe is dipped in blood, even before the supposed war. That's because the blood is *His own*.

"Who is this coming from Edom…with his garments stained crimson? Who is this, robed in splendor, striding forward in the greatness of his strength? 'It is I, proclaiming victory, mighty to save.' Why are your garments red, like those of one treading the winepress? 'I have trodden the winepress alone'" (Isaiah 63:1–3 NIV).

In Isaiah's day, they were certain the Messiah would trod the winepress in wrath and vengeance. But Jesus had already dealt with wrath *before creation* by bearing it. *They simply didn't know it yet.* Do you remember the last meal Jesus ate with His disciples?

"And he took a cup, and when he had given thanks he gave it to them, saying, 'Drink of it, all of you, for this is my blood of the covenant, which is poured out for many for the forgiveness of sins'" (Matthew 26:27–28).

The cross was the winepress. And He trod the winepress alone. And now, He appeared in a robe stained *in His own blood*, that we would take and drink, for the forgiveness of sins.

You might be thinking, Wait a minute—what about the sword? Doesn't Jesus come back swinging?

I'm glad you remembered. But also remember, Revelation is a book of images. And when Jesus returns, the sword isn't in His hand. It's coming from His mouth. Why? Because He *is* the sword.

"In the beginning was the Word...and the Word became flesh" (John 1:1, 14).

The word of God is "sharper than any two-edged sword, piercing to the division of soul and of spirit, of joints and of marrow, and discerning the thoughts and intentions of the heart" (Hebrews 4:12).

Jesus is the Sword of the Spirit—the Word who speaks over creation, separating once and for all our thoughts from our motives. And in this, He slays us all. "At the name of Jesus every knee should bow" (Philippians 2:10). For the waiting, the weary, and the wounded, the Sword brings healing; the longings for righteousness are finally fulfilled.

But for those who refuse to release the pride that violently assaults others, there is nowhere left to hide. Everything is seen for what it is. And our enemy, stripped of every disguise, must finally step from the shadows exposed as the vanquished coward he's always been. Brian Zahnd explains this powerfully. "Jesus overcame demonic evil by his word. Jesus said, 'Come out of the man, you evil spirit.' We might say Jesus waged war on demonic evil with the sword that came from his mouth. Jesus doesn't wield a sword in his hand to kill people; Jesus wields a sword from his mouth to set people free."[88]

The human race is finally receiving the last surgery we will ever need to be whole. And the sword is, in the end, revealed to be a surgeon's scalpel, not the artillery of an assassin.

Key 4: The Lion is a lamb

One final key reframes the image of our coming King, and it's found in Revelation 5.

John witnesses a mighty angel searching for someone worthy to open the scroll that holds the redemption of all things. But no one is found. Overcome with grief, John begins to weep until he hears an announcement that changes everything.

"Behold, the Lion of the tribe of Judah, the Root of David, has conquered, so that he can open the scroll" (Revelation 5:5).

A Lion. The image sends John's imagination rushing back to one of the earliest messianic prophecies.

"You are a lion's cub, Judah…the scepter will not depart from Judah…the obedience of the nations shall be his" (Genesis 49:9–10 NIV).

Yes, the *Lion of Judah* had come! The King from the promised tribe. The One with the right to rule. John braces himself for a vision of raw power. A great beast, wild and untouchable. He expects might. Intimidation. Fury.

But then he turns.

"And between the throne and the four living creatures and among the elders I saw a Lamb standing, as though it had been slain" (Revelation 5:6).

Instead of a roaring lion, he saw a slain lamb.

This is the great unveiling. The Lion is a Lamb.

Jesus didn't begin with non-violence only to pivot at the close of history. He never called an audible. From the very beginning, the power of God has been *sacrificial love.* He bore our wounds. He descended into our pain, not with a sword in His hand, but with scars on His body.

Because violence will never drive out violence.

Only love can do that.

What if…?

What if when we gaze upon Jesus on the cross, we see a God who would rather die than kill his enemies and who invites us to *be imitators* of that same love?

What if the enemy's empire falls by compassion not coercion? Love not legalism. Tapestries of hope not threats of hell.

What if God's answer for our emptiness was to empty Himself, and this empties hell of its power, filling us with His hope forever?

What if rather than bracing for the world to go to hell in a handbasket, we bring heaven to earth through hands that bask in His glory?

What if God isn't waiting to empty the earth in some Uber ride rapture to heaven but desires for His sons and daughters to empty themselves on earth, so heaven comes down?

What if the violent, pulpit-pounding, turn-or-burn view of God is not worthy of the Father revealed in Jesus?

What if perfect love actually does cast out fear?

What if...?

DISCUSSION QUESTIONS

1. When you think of the wrath of God, what images or emotions come to mind? How does seeing wrath as God's passionate opposition to everything that destroys love change the way you understand His heart and your own response to sin?
2. If Revelation is the unveiling of Jesus rather than a coded prediction of the end, what do you think God most wants us to see in it? How would reading Revelation through the lens of the Lamb change the way you approach both fear and hope about the future?
3. If Jesus conquers as the Lamb through humility, mercy, and sacrificial love, what does that say about the kind of power His followers are called to display in the world today?

ELEVEN

"JUST RIGHT"

How Jesus holds justice and mercy as one

"MERCY WITHOUT JUSTICE is the mother of dissolution; justice without mercy is cruelty" (Thomas Aquinas).[89]

Remember the old story of *Goldilocks and the Three Bears*? Long before kids could virtually carjack strangers in *Grand Theft Auto*, we had Goldilocks, an early icon of juvenile delinquency. You know the story. A little girl named Goldilocks stumbles upon an empty home in the woods. She breaks in, raids the pantry, vandalizes the furniture, and then passes out in someone else's bed.

With each violation, Goldie isn't satisfied until she finds the one that's just right.

The first porridge? Too hot. The second? Too cold. The third? *Just right.* The first chair? Too hard. The second? Too soft. The third? *Just right.* The first bed? Too firm. The second? Too floppy. The third? *Just right.*

By the time she drifts off to sleep, Goldie has eaten all the food, messed up all the beds, and shattered the chair of a toddler. And she doesn't care. Goldilocks is living her best life—until she wakes up to discover she's broken into the den of three bears. Now, if I had my way, this story would end with something like...And then Mama Bear said to Papa Bear, "Hold my earrings," as she proceeded to do what any Mama Bear does when someone comes between her and her cubs. The moral of the story: bad things happen when kids don't keep their hands to themselves and go places they shouldn't go. Stay in school and sweet dreams!

Something in us wants that ending. We're hardwired to long for injustice to be remedied. We want those who break the rules to get what's coming to them. We talk a lot about peace and love, but when someone invades our space, takes our stuff, or breaks our things, most of us desire payback far more than we'd like to admit.

But there's a way this story helps us. When it comes to how we believe God deals with injustice, opinions abound. Some who claim the name of Christ have embraced a kind of triumphalism—a sick delight when one's enemies get what's coming to them. They are quick to talk about the multitudes who will face danger on the day of judgment, yet strangely silent about their own responsibility to pursue those they claim to pity. They are the proud, card-carrying members of what I like to call the *Too-Hard Club*, a group convinced that the gospel must be shielded from the messiness of grace. Not surprising, they're also the least likely to orient their lives toward anyone outside their self-righteous fishbowls, content to swim only with those who look (and sin) exactly like themselves.

Meanwhile, another group, often well-meaning followers of Jesus, leans toward the opposite extreme. They extend a gospel that's far too soft. Eager to silence anything that even sounds like judgment, they work overtime to assure everyone that everything will be great no matter how we choose to live because God is Love. But in the wake of what amounts to syrupy self-actualization slogans that masquerade as spirituality, countless souls are left to perish for a lack of truth.

Somewhere between these two distortions, we meet Jesus doing what He always does in a polarized this or that world. *He offers another way.*

If we'd only look up, we'd see Jesus inviting us to leave the crowds of the extreme right and the extreme left, to enter through the narrow gate. Here we join Him in the life-giving tension that exists between our present concepts of justice and mercy. And only here will we adopt a posture that is just right for His kingdom to come.

DEFINING JUSTICE

If we're going to understand how justice fits into the story of redemption, we need to begin with two essential truths.

First, justice is *everywhere* in the Bible. It's not a side theme, it's central. More than 1,600 verses directly reference justice, describing how God responds to brokenness in the world and moves to set things right. That doesn't even include the many stories where people cry out for justice, where God promises to act justly, or where the faithful praise Him for bringing beauty from ashes. Justice isn't a footnote; it's a fingerprint, pressed onto nearly every page of Scripture.

Second, biblical justice is not a one-dimensional concept. It's a layered, multifaceted masterpiece. The Spirit-inspired authors didn't flatten God's justice into a caricature of wrath or sentimentality, crudely scribbled in crayons. Instead, they painted with care and complexity, adding layer upon layer like a master artist shading a canvas to reveal a work of genius.

We see a similar dynamic with our word *love*. In English, we use the same word to describe wildly different affections. I love pizza. I love my grandma. I love my spouse. Hopefully not all in the same way! But the Greeks had four distinct words to reflect love's many nuances. They understood that some ideas are too rich for a single word.

Now consider this. To express God's justice in a way that does Him justice, the writers of Scripture used over thirty different Hebrew and Greek words. Biblical justice is that intricate.

Most scholars agree these terms can be grouped into three major themes, interwoven strands that together form the full tapestry of justice in the heart of God.

- Justice (How wrongs are made right).
- Righteousness (How right relationship is sustained).
- Judgment (How truth is revealed and upheld).

Understanding these will change the way we approach the Bible and the way we live in the world.

Justice

The most frequently used Old Testament word for justice is *mišpāṭ* (pronounced mish-pawt'), meaning "the process of rightly judging or deciding a case in order to preserve or restore justice."[90] It's not just a legal term. It's a relational one. At its heart, mišpāṭ, reveals a God who doesn't merely possess justice. He is justice itself. He doesn't watch from a distance. He enters in.

Mišpāṭ speaks of God's active, ongoing presence to deliver what is good, right, fair, and restorative across His creation. This is not justice as cold punishment but as intimate goodness. The Judge of all the earth stoops lowly, not only to correct what's broken, but to lift up the broken.

We see God's direct justice echo through Scripture.

- "Shall not the Judge of all the earth do what is just?" (Genesis 18:25).
- "All his ways are justice. A God of faithfulness…just and upright is he" (Deuteronomy 32:4).
- "The Lord secures justice for the poor and upholds the cause of the needy" (Psalm 140:12 NIV).
- "Therefore the Lord waits to be gracious to you…For the Lord is a God of justice" (Isaiah 30:18).
- "I will seek the lost, and I will bring back the strayed, and I will bind up the injured, and I will strengthen the weak…I will feed them in justice" (Ezekiel 34:16).

Many of us can testify to those divine moments when God met us in the dust and defended us when no one else could. What other system of faith dares to imagine the Creator Himself stooping in the dirt beside the downtrodden He formed? This is the miracle of mišpāṭ.

But it doesn't stop there.

God also enacts mišpāṭ through His people. He fills us with His Spirit and commissions us as agents of restoration. True spiritual authority looks like humble hearts knit to the Father's, willing to champion justice. This was Israel's sacred calling.

- "Cursed is anyone who withholds justice from the foreigner, the fatherless or the widow" (Deuteronomy 27:19 NIV).
- "Learn to do good; seek justice, correct oppression; bring justice to the fatherless, plead the widow's cause" (Isaiah 1:17).
- "He has told you, O man, what is good; and what does the Lord require of you but to do justice, and to love kindness, and to walk humbly with your God?" (Micah 6:8).

Israel failed that calling. So have we. But God's justice does not hinge on our perfection. Through Isaiah, God made a promise of a coming King, one who would embody mišpāṭ in its fullness.

"Here is my servant, whom I uphold, my chosen one in whom I delight; I will put my Spirit on him, and he will bring justice to the nations. He will not shout or cry out, or raise his voice in the streets. A bruised reed he will not break, and a smoldering wick he will not snuff out. In faithfulness he will bring forth justice; he will not falter or be discouraged till he establishes justice on earth. In his teaching the islands will put their hope" (Isaiah 42:1–4 NIV).

Justice, in the hands of Jesus is not a hammer to punish but a hand to heal. Not distant judgment but intimate restoration. Not a courtroom ruling. An incarnate rescue.

Righteousness

The second thread woven through the tapestry of biblical justice is righteousness, anchored in two powerful words, sadîq and dikaiosynē.

The Hebrew word *ṣadîq* means, "what is just, lawful, and right."[91] The Greek word *dikaiosynē* means, "the state of a person as they were always meant to be."[92] While justice highlights what God does, righteousness reveals who God is, and who we are called to become in Him.

The Bible makes four foundational declarations about righteousness.

Declaration 1: God is righteous.

Righteousness is not simply a virtue God has; it is who He is. He always does what is right, faithful, and good over all He has created.

- "Your righteousness, O God, reaches the high heavens. You who have done great things, O God, who is like you?" (Psalm 71:19).
- "The Lord is righteous in all his ways and kind in all his works" (Psalm 145:17).
- "Righteous are you, O Lord, when I...plead my case before you" (Jeremiah 12:1).
- "Fear not, for I am with you; be not dismayed, for I am your God; I will strengthen you, I will help you, I will uphold you with my righteous right hand" (Isaiah 41:10).
- "For Christ is the end of the law for righteousness to everyone who believes" (Romans 10:4).

God cannot sin. He cannot be unjust, cruel, or indifferent. His righteousness is the guarantee that He will always act with perfect love and truth.

Declaration 2: We are not righteous in ourselves.

Though deeply unpopular in the age of pep talks to believe in yourself, the testimony of Scripture and our own conscience confirms, when left to ourselves, we are not as we should be.

- "There is no one on earth who is righteous, no one who does what is right and never sins" (Ecclesiastes 7:20 NIV).
- "None is righteous, no not one; no one understands; no one seeks for God. All have turned aside; together they have become worthless; no one does good, not even one" (Romans 3:10–12).
- "'All of us have become like one who is unclean, and all our righteous acts are like filthy rags...No one calls on your name or strives to lay hold of you'" (Isaiah 64:6–7 NIV).

We don't just need a kind God. We need a new heart. Our brokenness requires more than a divine philanthropist. We need a soul surgeon.

Declaration 3: Righteousness is a gift.

The gospel isn't merely that our sins are forgiven; it's that the righteousness of Christ has been imparted to us. Through Jesus, we have been made righteous.

"For Christ also suffered once for sins, the righteous for the unrighteous, to bring you to God. He was put to death in the body but made alive in the Spirit" (1 Peter 3:18 NIV).

"Abraham believed God, and it was counted to him as righteousness" (Romans 4:3).

"I do not set aside the grace of God, for if righteousness could be gained through the law, Christ died for nothing!" (Galatians 2:21 NIV).

"You have been set free from sin and have become slaves to righteousness" (Romans 6:18 NIV).

The scandal and beauty of the gospel is that God doesn't just cover our brokenness. He makes us new. And then calls us to live that way.

Declaration 4: Righteousness is a life of restorative love.

True righteousness doesn't end with personal piety. It flows outward into justice, compassion, and action. The righteous are those who courageously step into all that is not yet right in the world, bringing restoration in Jesus' name.

- "'Seek first the kingdom of God and his righteousness'" (Matthew 6:33).
- "We are therefore Christ's ambassadors, as though God were making his appeal through us. We implore you on Christ's behalf: Be reconciled to God. God made him who had no sin to be sin for us, so that in him we might become the righteousness of God" (2 Corinthians 5:20–21 NIV).
- "A harvest of righteousness is sown in peace by those who make peace" (James 3:18).

To reduce righteousness to mere belief, behavior, or doctrine is to distort it. If righteousness doesn't move your hands and feet, it has likely not gripped your heart. The righteous are not those who isolate or insulate themselves from a broken world, but those who refuse to look away from the cries of poverty, neglect, abuse, and injustice, choosing instead to step forward as ministers of reconciliation.

Scripture links righteousness and justice seventy-four times. They are divine companions, justice in action, righteousness in character.

- "For the Lord is righteous, he loves justice" (Psalm 11:7 NIV).
- "Your righteousness is like the highest mountains, your justice like the great deep" (Psalm 36:6 NIV).
- "Righteousness and justice are the foundation of your throne" (Psalm 89:14).
- "The Lord works righteousness and justice for all the oppressed" (Psalm 103:6).
- "My righteousness draws near...my arm will bring justice to the nations" (Isaiah 51:5 NIV).
- "I will betroth you in righteousness and justice, in love and compassion" (Hosea 2:19b NIV).
- "Let justice roll down like waters, and righteousness like an ever-flowing stream" (Amos 5:24).

Righteousness is not just right living. It's right loving. It is the God-breathed identity we receive in Christ. And the world-shaping mission we embody through Him.

Judgment

To complete the biblical portrait of justice, we must consider a third and essential facet, judgment.

If righteousness reflects God's character and justice His compassion, judgment reveals God's commitment to cleanse the world of evil once and for all. It is the day when wrongs are righted, hidden things are revealed, and every cry for justice is answered in full.

The primary Hebrew word is *šāpaṭ*, "meaning to judge, to govern rightly, to execute justice, to vindicate wrongdoing."[93] Its Greek counterpart *krinō* means, "to separate, discern, decide, or issue a verdict."[94] Together, they describe God's work of bringing truth into the light and setting all things in their rightful place.

British theologian Oliver O'Donovan explains, "To judge is to make a distinction between the just and the unjust, or more precisely, to bring the distinction which already exists between them into the light of public observation."[95]

In this sense, judgment is God revealing reality for what it truly is. It is not arbitrary punishment or a divine outburst of rage. Judgment unveils what has always been, seen through the eyes of perfect righteousness and administered with unwavering justice.

The Bible points to this future moment with hope, not dread.

- "Let all creation rejoice before the Lord, for he comes, he comes to judge the earth. He will judge the world in righteousness and the peoples in his faithfulness" (Psalm 96:13 NIV).
- "God will judge the righteous and the wicked, for there is a time for every matter and for every work" (Ecclesiastes 3:17).
- "Because he has fixed a day on which he will judge the world in righteousness by a man whom he has appointed [Jesus]; and of this he has given assurance to all by raising him from the dead" (Acts 17:31).

Yes, a day is coming, a day when every injustice will be answered, when the enemy of our souls will be sentenced forever. The eternal King will wipe all our tears and welcome us into a kingdom where justice rolls on like the Mississippi River, and sorrow ceases to exist (John 16:11, Revelation 21:4).

That said, the Bible also records many moments when the cries of the oppressed rise before heaven in the here and now, reaching a breaking point where God's justice steps in as a voice for the voiceless.

It was this cry of enslaved Israelites that led to their deliverance in the Exodus. It is this cry of the vulnerable that echoes throughout the Law, the Prophets, and the Psalms.[96]

And it is this same cry that leads to one of the Bible's most sobering stories of Sodom and Gomorrah.

"Because the outcry against Sodom and Gomorrah is great and their sin is very grave, I will go down to see whether they have done altogether according to the outcry that has come to me" (Genesis 18:20–21).

Space does not permit a complete treatment, but Genesis and the later prophets paint a devastating picture of these cities. Their culture was marked by exploitation of the vulnerable, sexual brutality, extreme greed, and a hardened refusal to show compassion to the poor. Arrogant, abusive, overfed, and unconcerned, they became poster children of pride that erupts into violence.[97]

And yet, even here we see the remarkable patience of the God who comes low. As God draws near to rescue the oppressed, He expresses a willingness to spare the entire city if even ten righteous people can be found. Such a remnant would reveal the faintest hope that the oppressors were not beyond repentance. A single spark of righteousness would have preserved a city.

But none were found.

For the sake of Abraham, God reached down to rescue his family—six in total. But before they could leave, Lot's sons-in-law defected, laughing at the idea of abandoning the sin they had grown to call home. As Lot and his daughters fled the city, his wife lingered behind before finally turning back to her own demise. In my mind's eye, I can almost see God standing on the edge of the city, urgently reaching for her hand to lead her out of Sodom, but she was unwilling to let Sodom leave her heart.

The story is tragic, but it again reveals the rescuing heart of God. He is merciful, and He is just.

The Bible never presents judgment as God losing control. It reveals God stepping in with the mercy denied to the suffering, refusing to allow those who have destroyed themselves to destroy the world He loves. The question is not if there will be judgment, but how God's judgment will be carried out.

And that's where Jesus steps in.

The cross is God's judgment.

If we miss this, we miss the heart of the gospel. The cross is God's judgment against sin. It's not that God will deal with sin one day. He *has* dealt with it, once and for all, when He carried its full weight upon His own shoulders. Outside the city gates, Jesus bore it, condemned it, and broke its power in His own flesh.

"There is now no condemnation for those who are in Christ Jesus, because through Christ Jesus the law of the Spirit who gives life has set you free from the law of sin and death. For what the law was powerless to do... God did by sending his own Son in the likeness of sinful flesh to be a sin offering. And so he condemned sin in the flesh, in order that the righteous requirement of the law might be fully met in us, who do not live according to the flesh but according to the Spirit" (Romans 8:1–4 NIV).

God condemned sin within Himself—taking its judgment upon His own body on the cross. This is how Jesus could truthfully say, "For God did not send his Son into the world to condemn [krinō, judge] the world, but in order that the world might be saved through him" (John 3:17).

The incarnation was not an angry dad bursting in to catch us in our sin. It was a rescue mission. And on the cross, Jesus delivered the final verdict: "It is finished" (see John 19:30). The penalty of sin, the power of death, and the grip of injustice were broken forever.

And yet, in the very next verse, Jesus added a sobering twist when He proclaimed, "Whoever believes in him is not condemned, but whoever does not believe is condemned [krinō, judged] already, because he has not believed in the name of the only Son of God" (John 3:18).

Judgment is real. But God's basis of judgment isn't measured by how many Bible facts we can recite or how well we perform our moral routines. It's about what we will do with the judgment Christ took on our behalf. Will we receive what God has done for us or insist on standing as our own defense attorney? In our post-Enlightenment world, we've confused knowing about God with knowing Him. Some who could ace every theology exam will be stunned to hear Him say, "I never knew you" (see Matthew 7:23). And many others, written off as too messy or too wrong, will be found kneeling closer to the throne than anyone expected.

What then, is our role in judgment?

God has promised He will judge all things fairly. But when it comes to our role in judgment, Jesus is direct.

- "Do not judge, and you will not be judged. Do not condemn, and you will not be condemned. Forgive, and you will be forgiven" (Luke 6:37 NIV).
- "You, therefore, have no excuse, you who pass judgment on someone else, for at whatever point you judge another, you are condemning yourself, because you who pass judgment do the same things. Now we know that God's judgment against those who do such things is based on truth. So when you, a mere human being, pass judgment on them and yet do the same things, do you think you will escape God's judgment? Or do you show contempt for the riches of his kindness, forbearance and patience, not realizing that God's kindness is intended to lead you to repentance?" (Romans 2:1–4 NIV).
- "Who are you to judge someone else's servant? To their own master, servants stand or fall. And they will stand, for the Lord is able to make them stand" (Romans 14:4 NIV).
- "Therefore do not pronounce judgment before the time, before the Lord comes, who will bring to light the things now hidden in darkness and will disclose the purposes of the heart. Then each one will receive his commendation from God" (1 Corinthians 4:5).
- "Anyone who speaks against a brother or sister or judges them speaks against the law and judges it. When you judge the law, you are not keeping it, but sitting in judgment on it. There is only one Lawgiver and Judge, the one who is able to save and destroy. But you—who are you to judge your neighbor?" (James

4:11b–12 NIV).

In a recent Barna poll, people who identified with no religious faith were asked why they resisted Christianity. The top three answers are telling.

1. Hypocrisy of Christians.
2. Judgmental attitudes of Christians.
3. Political entanglements of Christians.[98]

By contrast, they held overwhelmingly positive views of Jesus. Let this sink in. People like Jesus; they just have a hard time seeing Him through the way we sometimes choose to live.

This isn't a new problem. The early church struggled with the same temptation to judge others quickly, to fill in gaps, or to assume the worst. But Jesus calls us to something higher.

First, we can resist the urge to categorize people. We don't know the story God is writing in someone's heart or what chapter He's presently on.

Second, we can spend our energy helping others encounter God's goodness. This is our true work. Zechariah wrote, "This is what the Lord Almighty said: 'Administer true justice; show mercy and compassion to one another'" (Zechariah 7:9 NIV).

So, how do we do that practically? That's what we'll explore in the rest of this chapter.

RESTORATIVE JUSTICE AND RECTIFYING JUSTICE

It may help to view God's justice through two interwoven lenses. We can refer to these as restorative justice and rectifying justice.

The dominant theme of Scripture is the restorative nature of justice—God's patient, persistent work to rescue, redeem, and restore everything that's been lost. It's the heartbeat of the kingdom. Whether we realize it or not, this justice constantly works in and around us. It's the glue of the universe, the breath of the Spirit in motion.

Restorative justice is…

- Forgiveness

- Pruning
- A Refiner's Fire
- Answered Prayer
- Repentance
- Grace
- Deliverance
- Anointing
- Discipline

This kind of justice draws us closer to God's heart and back into the wholeness we were created for. It restores. This is the 24/7 work of the kingdom, ongoing, redemptive, and resolute. Restorative justice is the thread that runs through the tapestry of Scripture.

"He who was seated on the throne said, 'Behold, I am making all things new!'" (Revelation 21:5).

"For as in Adam all die, so in Christ all will be made alive" (1 Corinthians 15:22).

"The Lord…is patient toward you, not wishing that any should perish, but that all should reach repentance" (2 Peter 3:9).

The unapologetic aim of the King is not punishment, but restoration. We are longing for a world remade where heaven once again kisses earth. And yet, Scripture also speaks of a sobering reality. God's rectifying justice removes what refuses to be redeemed. This is not a contradiction to His character but a fulfillment of it. When sin and violence persist, unrepentant and corrosive, God acts, not out of rage, but righteousness.

In Revelation 20, we're given a vivid glimpse.

"The dead were judged according to what they had done…and death and Hades were thrown into the lake of fire" (Revelation 20:12c, 14 NIV).

Isaiah calls this kind of justice God's *strange work*, not because it's unjust, but because it is alien to His deepest desire. In Isaiah 28, God pleads with Israel, who once again placed their trust in political alliances over divine mercy, choosing Egypt to protect them from Assyria instead of God. Through the prophet, He declared:

"See, I lay a stone in Zion, a tested stone, a precious cornerstone for a sure foundation; the one who relies on it will never be stricken with panic. I will make justice the measuring line and righteousness the plumb line; hail will sweep away your refuge, the lie, and water will overflow your hiding place. Your covenant with death will be annulled; your agreement with the realm of the dead will not stand. When the overwhelming scourge sweeps by, you will be beaten down by it…The Lord will rise up as he did at Mount Perazim, he will rouse himself as in the Valley of Gibeon—to do his work, his strange work, and perform his task, his alien task" (Isaiah 28:16–18, 21 NIV).

Notice the kindness of God's pursuit and the gravity of our response. The cornerstone sent for salvation would become a *scourge* for those who refused it. It is as Jesus said, "the one who falls on this stone will be broken to pieces" (Matthew 21:44). God's judgment isn't a sudden outburst. It's heartbreak. He longed to be their foundation, but they found shelter in lies. Even the promised rectifying justice was wrapped in divine mercy. It is strange to God, quite literally. In the Hebrew, this word means "foreign, alien, unfamiliar, and loathsome."[99] Love will do what is just and right, even when it breaks its own heart.

Later, God spoke through Ezekiel with raw emotion.

"Therefore, you Israelites, I will judge each of you according to your own ways, declares the Sovereign Lord. Repent! Turn away from all your offenses; then sin will not be your downfall. Rid yourselves of all the offenses you have committed, and get a new heart and a new spirit. Why will you die, people of Israel? For I take no pleasure in the death of anyone, declares the Sovereign Lord. Repent and live!" (Ezekiel 18:30–32 NIV).

This is the God we meet in Scripture—a Father who warns because He longs to restore. He delays judgment not out of weakness, but because He is giving time for mercy to win. He is not a distant deity but a near and present God, inviting us to lay down our violence so we might enter the world to come.

God will make all things new. But not everything *wants* to relinquish the corruption it has grown to love. In the world to come, there will be no room for violence. We have to let it go.

Violence cannot RSVP for the coming kingdom

We return one final time to the prophet Isaiah and the vision God entrusted to him, a vision not of escape but of fulfillment. Jesus proclaims this kingdom and invites us to live it—here and now, as peacemakers and ambassadors of His reign. In this unveiled future, violence and injustice are conspicuously absent. They simply have no seat at the table.

"Many peoples will come and say, 'Come, let us go up to the mountain of the Lord, to the temple of the God of Jacob. He will teach us his ways, so that we may walk in his paths.' The law will go out from Zion, the word of the Lord from Jerusalem. He will judge between the nations and will settle disputes for many peoples. They will beat their swords into plowshares and their spears into pruning hooks. Nation will not take up sword against nation, nor will they train for war anymore" (Isaiah 2:3–4 NIV).

Isaiah also prophesied, "The wolf will live with the lamb...The infant will play near the cobra's den...They will neither harm nor destroy on all my holy mountain, for the earth will be filled with the knowledge of the Lord as the waters cover the sea" (Isaiah 11:6, 8–9). His prophecy paints a picture of creation fully restored, where peace is not just possible, it's permanent.

The heart of God beats for restoration—for a justice that makes all things whole. But violence, pride, and injustice cannot RSVP to the party. They will not pass through the gates. Not because God excludes, but because they refuse to be transformed.

And so, we arrive at this moment in history, *our moment*, where God still waits with outstretched arms, pleading with His creation to let Him annul our covenant with death before the floodwaters of injustice are swept away forever. God hates separation. It is alien to His nature. But He will not violate our freedom to love or to leave. As wild as it sounds, people can resist His kindness, clinging with white-knuckled defiance to the empire of self. But to do so, one must drown out the music of heaven. They must close their ears to the whispers of mercy. And blind their eyes to the relentless pursuit of a God who still walks every day in the Garden, asking, "Where are you?"

Is it possible to reject Him, or like Lot's wife, refuse to evict violence from our hearts? *Yes*. But what soul has truly tasted the goodness of God only to choose to turn away? Most often, what people resist isn't *Him*, it's a shattered image, distorted by bad theology and broken mirrors. Jesus said the fields are white for harvest. And love still sends us—not to punish, but to restore.

DISCUSSION QUESTIONS:

1. Where do you tend to lean in your view of God's nature—toward justice or mercy? How has your upbringing, church background, or personal experience shaped the way you understand God's justice?
2. What does it look like for followers of Jesus to pursue restorative justice today? Can you identify a situation in your life, your church, or the broader world where God might be inviting you to help turn brokenness into healing?
3. Isaiah called God's rectifying justice a *strange work*. Why do you think this kind of judgment grieves God's heart, even when it's just? What does this reveal about the character of God, and how should it shape the way we engage people we see as wrong or lost.

TWELVE

JUSTICE AS RESTORATIVE LOVE

How the Father draws near to defend, deliver, and disciple His kids

IN THE PREVIOUS chapter, we explored the layered beauty of God's justice, allowing the light of Christ to illuminate its many facets. We traced a holy triad (justice, righteousness, and judgment) revealing a God who consistently steps into our brokenness to make all things new. We discovered that while restorative justice, God's active work to heal, redeem, and restore, is His constant pursuit, rectifying justice is His strange work—a last resort, never His desire for any son or daughter.

Now, we turn from the theological to the tangible. In this chapter, we'll examine three practical ways God brings justice near to us, not as punishment, but as a means for maturing love. We'll see how the Father draws close to defend, deliver, and disciple His kids, and how He invites us to join Him in this work upon the earth.

JUSTICE AS RESTORATIVE LOVE THAT DEFENDS THE DEFENSELESS

God is a good Father who answers the cries of His children. As a dad of five, I've heard my share of cries over the years—loud, dramatic, and echoing from the far corners of our house. Most of the time, they're just noisy complaints. Someone didn't share the toy, didn't play fair, or didn't get their way. And let's be honest, those cries aren't exactly compassion magnets. Whining is like fingernails on the chalkboard of my heart; it makes me want to run in the other direction.

But then there's another kind of cry.

The real kind. The kind born from fear, pain, or heartbreak.

The kind of cry that makes a parent move without thinking, activating something fierce and tender at the same time. This cry, you run to. God does too.

Ishmael, cast into the desert, wept as he lay dying. And God heard his cry and made the boy into a great nation (Genesis 21:17).

The Israelites, beaten and enslaved under Egypt's regime, groaned for rescue. And the Lord heard their cry, setting them free and giving them a story that would echo across eternity (Exodus 3:7).

David, hunted like an animal by the most powerful man in the nation, cried from the caves. And God heard his cry, lifting him to the throne (2 Samuel 22:7).

Elijah, heartbroken beside a widow's lifeless son, lifted his voice. And God heard his cry, raising the boy and revealing His mercy to the Gentiles (1 Kings 17:22).

The victims of Sodom, long silenced under abuse, groaned under oppression. And God heard their cry, bringing an end to their torment (Genesis 19:13).

From Genesis to Revelation, the refrain resounds. Every time we cry, God hears. And every time God hears, He moves.

- "The Lord is near to all who call on him…he also hears their cry and saves them" (Psalm 145:18–19).
- "Evening, morning and noon I cry out…and he hears my voice" (Psalm 55:17 NIV).
- "O Lord, you hear the desire of the afflicted…you will incline your ear to do justice to the fatherless and the oppressed" (Psalm 10:17–18).
- "When righteous cry for help, the Lord hears…The Lord is near

to the brokenhearted" (Psalm 34:17–18).

This is not wishful thinking. This is justice as God defines it. A defender who stands *with* the overlooked, the outnumbered, and the unheard.

And when His children cry, He doesn't walk away.

He comes running.

Justice as restorative love that answers the cry of the vulnerable

One of the most vital and overlooked aspects of God's justice is His unwavering nearness to the vulnerable—the forgotten, the marginalized, the enslaved, the despised, the lonely, the weak, and the sinner. In Matthew 25, Jesus pulled back the curtain on the day of judgment and painted a picture that upends our assumptions. As a Shepherd separating sheep from goats, He distinguished them not by their theology or moral precision, but by one thing. How they responded to the cries of the least.

"The King will say to those on his right, 'Come, you who are blessed by my Father, inherit the kingdom prepared for you from the foundation of the world. For I was hungry and you gave me food, I was thirsty and you gave me drink, I was a stranger and you welcomed me, I was naked and you clothed me, I was sick and you visited me, I was in prison and you came to me.'

"Then the righteous will answer him, saying, 'Lord, when did we see you hungry and feed you, or thirsty and give you drink? And when did we see you a stranger and welcome you, or naked and clothe you? And when did we see you sick or in prison and visit you?' And the King will answer them, 'Truly I say to you, as you did it to one of the least of these my brothers, you did it to me'" (Matthew 25:34–40).

Jesus went on to describe the judgment of the goats—those who could not recognize Him in the faces of the hungry, the poor, and the forgotten.

"Then he will say to those on his left, 'Depart from me, you cursed, into the eternal fire prepared for the devil and his angels. For I was hungry and you gave me no food, I was thirsty and you gave me no drink, I was a stranger and you did not welcome me, naked and you did not clothe me, sick and in prison and you did not visit me.' Then they also will answer, saying, 'Lord, when did we see you hungry or thirsty or a stranger or naked or sick or in prison, and did not minister to you?' Then he will answer them, saying, 'Truly, I say to you, as you did not do it to one of the least of these, you did not do it to me'" (Matthew 25:41–45).

The difference between the sheep and the goats wasn't measured by creeds or by conduct. They weren't separated based on what TV shows they watched, how often they went to church, or how many cuss words they dropped. The dividing line was drawn by one question. What did they do with the cry of the vulnerable?

Let's consider the categories Jesus names:

Hungry: Those with deep, gnawing need—physical, emotional, or spiritual.[100]

Thirsty: Those who feel parched for worth, weary from lack, longing for refreshment.[101]

Stranger: The alienated, the outsider, the overlooked—whether foreigner, outcast, or orphaned heart.[102]

Naked: The exposed and ashamed, stripped of dignity or voice, longing to be clothed in compassion.[103]

Sick: The weakened and worn—by illness, mental anguish, addiction, or deep soul fatigue.[104]

Imprisoned: Those trapped, confined by bars of circumstance, shame, or spiritual oppression.[105]

Notice, *Jesus offers no qualifications.* He doesn't say, "Blessed are you for helping the *innocent* poor and the *wrongly* accused." He does not differentiate between the deserving and the undeserving. His kingdom doesn't run background checks. It runs on radical, restorative love.

This is the staggering scandal of God's justice. It defends the defenseless, even when their wounds are partly self-inflicted. It draws near to the broken, not because they earned it, but because they are beloved. And Jesus says, shockingly, that our response to them is our response to *Him.*

The kingdom of God is not built on status or theology alone, but on love in motion—love that hears, love that feeds, love that visits, love that stays. Our truest worship of Jesus isn't sung in sanctuaries but shown in how we respond to the cries of the vulnerable. Of all the verses in Scripture, none is more familiar than John 3:16. Yet we often forget that when God so loved the world, His love didn't stop at its brightest or most beautiful parts.

For God so loved…

- the ones walking in darkness and those hiding in shame,
- the suffering and the shunned,
- the dirty, the starving, the hurting, the immigrant,
- the second-class, the sick, the diseased, the prisoner,
- the unspectacular, the unschooled, the unqualified,
- the unable, the unclean, the unstable,
- the oppressed and the oppressor,
- the wealthy and the poor,
- the powerful, the greedy, the dishonest,
- the religious and the self-righteous,
- the violent and the vengeful,
- the insecure, the jealous, the petty,
- the sexually broken, the disobedient, the guilty, the caught, the shamed,
- the addict, the anxious, the exhausted,
- the disqualified, the ordinary, the invisible, the written-off,
- the demonized, the pagan, the traitor, the beggar,
- the hopeless and the voiceless,
- the lame, the leper, the lost, the least, the last,
- the adulterer, the sinner, the mourning, the persecuted, and even the persecutor,
- the misunderstood, the outcast, the lonely, the slow to learn,
- the world.

Justice as restorative love that delivers the unjust from the accuser

God is a gracious Father who pursues us in our prodigal ways. One of the most stunning aspects of God's justice is this: He draws near not only to the oppressed, but also to the oppressor. The One who hears the cries of the wounded also longs to rescue the one wielding the sword. God reveals His justice not just in defending the defenseless but in transforming the unjust into new creations.

The Bible is full of such stories.

Saul the persecutor becomes Paul the preacher.

Zacchaeus the cheat becomes Zacchaeus the charitable.

Moses the law-breaking wanderer becomes Moses the law-giving father.

Mary Magdalene, from perfectly bound to perfectly found.

The woman at the well, from reviled to revivalist.

Rahab, from harlot to holy host.

Scripture never divides humanity into tidy categories of good guys and bad guys. In reality, there are only *living* guys and *dead* guys. And every one of us were among the dead—cut off and incapable of saving ourselves (Ephesians 2:1–9). If we're honest, we have to admit we were far more like the bad guys, enemies of God whom He still moved toward in mercy (Romans 5:10). This is justice as deliverance. God's refusal to give up on those who've wandered far.

"Opponents must be gently instructed, in the hope…that they will come to their senses and escape from the trap of the devil, who has taken them captive to do his will" (2 Timothy 2:25–26 NIV).

"Good and upright is the Lord; therefore he instructs sinners in his ways" (Psalm 25:8 NIV).

Delivering justice confronts those in rebellion, not to condemn them, but to redeem them. It's what sent Moses to plead with Pharaoh, even as Pharaoh's heart grew hard.[106] It's what moved God to spare Nineveh, sending Jonah to offer mercy rather than wrath. *Delivering justice* led Him to raise up judges for a backslidden Israel. And it's what caused Him to pursue one of Israel's most brutal enemies: King Nebuchadnezzar. God's *delivering justice* comes low to those positioned in opposition to His kingdom plans, not to wipe them out, but so they can repent and be changed.

He is able to humble.

Nebuchadnezzar, ruler of Babylon, destroyed Jerusalem, desecrated the temple, and enslaved God's people. The only thing looming larger than Nebuchadnezzar's power was his ego, which led him to build a ninety-foot golden idol used to demand worship. But when three faithful Israelites refused, he had them thrown into a furnace, only to be met by a fourth figure in the flames, one *like a Son of God* (Daniel 3:25 NKJV). The fire didn't consume them. Not even their clothes were singed.

The pre-incarnate Christ entered the fire, not to kill Nebuchadnezzar, but to reveal a better kingdom. And *for a moment*, the king's eyes opened. He praised the God of Israel.

But old empires die hard. Soon, Nebuchadnezzar returned to comfort and control. God gave him a disturbing dream, and Daniel delivered its meaning. Turn from your injustice. Stop oppressing the poor. Humble yourself, or judgment will come.

"Break off your sins by practicing righteousness, and your iniquities by showing mercy to the oppressed, that there may perhaps be a lengthening of your prosperity" (Daniel 4:27).

God waited twelve months for him to repent. But he wouldn't. And so, judgment came, not as fire or flood, but in giving the king over to his own broken thoughts. His mind unraveled. His kingdom crumbled. And still, God didn't give up. Even in judgment, God was delivering the unjust, showing Nebuchadnezzar the path home.

Eventually, the king awoke from his madness, humbled, and healed. He would go on to write, "Now I, Nebuchadnezzar, praise and extol and honor the King of heaven, for all his works are right and his ways are just; and those who walk in pride he is able to humble" (Daniel 4:37).

This is *delivering justice*. Not retribution, but restoration. Not getting the bad guys so the good guys win, but about raising all of us to life.

But what about vengeance?

Some may object, quoting Hebrews 10:30, "Vengeance is mine." But we would be wise to take note of two important truths: First, if vengeance belongs to *God*, then it never belongs to *us*. We're not qualified to wield it without turning it into a weapon for pride, pain, or self-preservation. And second, let's consider what God did with His vengeance. He bore it. The One with every right to repay His enemies chose instead to be nailed to a cross by them, and for them. He cried, "Father, *forgive* them" (Luke 23:34, emphasis mine). In doing so, Jesus declared, "Vengeance is mine" as He took it upon Himself.

Yes, people can resist the justice that delivers. Like Pharaoh, they can harden their hearts to the end. But it will be a slow spiritual suicide, one inch at a time, turning away from mercy until they no longer recognize their own reflection. C.S. Lewis puts it hauntingly well.

"It is a serious thing...to remember that the dullest and most uninteresting person you talk to may one day be a creature which, if you saw it now, you would be strongly tempted to worship, or else a horror and a corruption such as you now meet, if at all, only in a nightmare. All day long we are, in some degree, helping each other to one or other of these destinations."[107]

And that's why, for the follower of Jesus, the path is clear.

As long as it is day, we go low. We keep forgiving. We speak truth in love. We do not give up. We do everything in our power to help even the hardest hearts see the face of the Father still inviting them home.

Because justice is restorative love that refuses to quit.

Justice as restorative love to disciple sons and daughters

God is a loving Father who trains His children toward maturity. The third expression of God's restorative justice is reserved for those who already trust Him as Father. It is *discipling justice*, His loving commitment to form us into maturity.

We turn to a passage many believers have quietly wished didn't exist—largely because of one uncomfortable word: Discipline.

"Have you completely forgotten this word of encouragement that addresses you as a father addresses his son? It says, 'My son, do not make light of the Lord's discipline, and do not lose heart when he rebukes you, because the Lord disciplines the one he loves, and he chastens everyone he accepts as his son'" (Hebrews 12:5–6 NIV).

It's striking that Hebrews calls discipline an encouragement. The word *encourage* means, "to place courage into someone." The Greek term is related to *Paraklesis*, the title Jesus gives the Holy Spirit, "Comforter, Helper, Advocate."[108] This discipline isn't harsh correction, but love that strengthens and equips.

Take a deep breath. We've all experienced forms of correction that were shaming or destructive. But God's discipline isn't punitive, it's paternal. And when we begin to trust this truth, it fills us with courage.

The word *discipline*, *paideia*, means "the full training and education of a child toward mature adulthood."[109] It's the shaping of intellect, character, passions, and purpose. It's where we get the word *discipleship*.

Sometimes discipline looks like the *wonder* of new revelation or skills learned.

Sometimes it feels like *stretching*, being called into something unfamiliar.

And sometimes it *stings*, when God rebukes us for our own good.

But all of it is love. A good Father trains His children because He wants to share His life with them.

An anemic view of love: Eli and his sons

Do you remember Eli in the Old Testament? He raised the prophet Samuel and was a priest in Israel. But Eli's failure as a father stands as a tragic warning.

His sons were worthless men (1 Samuel 2:12). They abused their spiritual authority, stealing sacrifices, threatening violence, and even committing sexual sin with women at the tent of meeting. Eli was grieved, and he confronted them saying, "Why do you do such things? I hear from all the people about these wicked deeds of yours. No, my sons; the report I hear spreading among the Lord's people is not good" (1 Samuel 2:23–24 NIV).

But here is the important key. After challenging his sons, Eli did nothing more. He had the authority to stop their injustice. And He did not. He offered words but withheld action. God's rebuke came clearly. "Why do you scorn my sacrifice…Why do you honor your sons more than me?" (1 Samuel 2:29 NIV).

Eli confused sentimentality for love. He chose to respect his sons' rights over doing what was right.

Proverbs 22:6 is often quoted as "Train up a child in the way he should go," but the Hebrew is better rendered, "Train a child in his own way (what he thinks is best), and when he is old, he will not depart from it." That's exactly what Eli did, relinquishing his responsibility as their father to shape his sons, letting them determine morality for themselves.

And his failure bore generational consequences.

A WEAK VIEW OF JUDGMENT: DAVID'S SILENCE AND THE COLLAPSE OF A KINGDOM

David, the man after God's own heart, reveals a deeper tragedy of what happens when a father chooses distance over discipline. The downfall of his family came to pass in several successive seasons of passivity.

The Rape of Tamar

David's son Amnon, in a fit of lust, raped his half-sister Tamar. David was furious, but he did nothing (2 Samuel 13:21). Tamar lived desolate, and her brother Absalom began plotting revenge.

The Murder of Amnon

For the next two years, Absalom hated his brother in his heart before giving vent to his rage and having Amnon killed. Again, David was silent. Though he longed for his son, he let him live in exile for three years (2 Samuel 13:38–39). When Absalom returned, David waited an additional two years before a tearful embrace. But this was no happy story. And it was about to get a lot worse.

The Rebellion of Absalom and Adonijah

Absalom eventually stole the kingdom and slept with David's concubines on the palace roof (2 Samuel 16:22). David fled again, doing nothing to intervene. In time, Absalom was killed in battle. Later, David's son Adonijah tried to seize the throne as well, but David had never confronted him. "His father had never at any time displeased him by asking, 'Why have you done thus and so?'" (1 Kings 1:6).

David was a worshiper, a warrior, and a king. But as a father, his silence sowed the seeds of sorrow that ripened into full-grown rebellion.

THE COURAGE TO EMBRACE GOD'S DISCIPLINE

Eli and David were good men. But they failed their children by refusing to step into the discomfort of *discipling discipline.* Many of us do the same, opting for politeness over truth, distance over growth, and shallow peace over holy transformation.

But our Father wants better for us. He loves us too much to leave us in immaturity.

God disciplines us for our good in order that we may share in his holiness. "No discipline seems pleasant at the time, but painful. Later on, however, it produces a harvest of righteousness and peace for those who have been trained by it" (Hebrews 12:11 NIV).

This is justice. Not punishment, but parenting—choosing to lean into the Spirit's training in your life with joy. He is shaping us, not just into wholeness, but into a worthier reflection of His image within us.

As we have seen, God's justice is not a single note but a beautiful, continual melody. It draws near to defend the defenseless, deliver the unjust, and disciple His children.

To walk in His way, we must reject the two great counterfeits of our age.

- The brash bravado of God, guns, and glory. This is a faith that delights in the downfall of its enemies and wields judgment like a weapon.
- The syrupy sentimentality of "Just Do You, Bro." This flattery leaves people enslaved to the fractured stories they've told themselves.

The first assaults spiritual orphans in the name of the Father. The second enshrines orphans as their own gods, leaving them bound in chains of self-destruction.

But there is a better way—the narrow way of love that Jesus calls us to walk.

Brian Zahnd reminds us, "The golden rule is the narrow gate. The narrow gate is not a sinner's prayer, the narrow gate is the practice of the Jesus way."[110]

We can step into the Jesus way right now by choosing to walk the narrow path between mercy and justice, loving God with our whole heart, and loving our neighbors as ourselves.

And so we declare:

We are those who *love* others as we long to be loved by the Father.

We are those who *forgive* others as we have been forgiven.

We are those who *bless* others when they curse us, for this is how the Father has *blessed* us.

In our hyper-reactive callout culture, where judgment is passed with the swipe of a finger and empathy runs thin, perhaps we should pause to ask a better question. What if this was your child?

How far would you go? How long would you wait? How many tears would you cry before giving up?

If you're a parent, you already know the answer. You wouldn't stop. You would love to the end. All of creation is made up of the children of that kind of Father. And *Jesus is His answer* to the question, How far would you go? He's still answering it, even now, as we cry, "How long, oh Lord?"

He's not being *slow*.

He's not being *unjust*.

He's simply pleading, pursuing, and patiently waiting, longing for hearts to soften at the sound of His voice.

God's justice is not vengeance dressed up in religious robes. It is His kingdom breaking in to restore peace, dignity, freedom, hope, and healing. God's justice draws near to wrap His presence around the world He loves.

For the child crying in the dark, justice looks like the Father's embrace.

For the refugee seeking shelter, justice provides a safe bed and open arms. For the narcissist, the abuser, and the oppressor, God's justice interrupts their ability to harm, neutralizing their cruelty so others may live. Yet even here, His mercy pleads for them to turn and come home.

We will all meet the same embrace. But we will not all experience it the same way. To the heart that longs to come home, it will be the warmth we've waited for all our lives. To the heart clutching its own throne, the wraparound presence of God will burn like fire. In the end, love will come for us all. And on that day, it's what we've loved that will determine whether it feels like a homecoming or a reckoning.

DISCUSSION QUESTIONS:

1. Which expression of God's restorative justice—defending the defenseless, delivering the unjust, or disciplining His children, was most challenging or clarifying for you? Why?
2. How have you seen yourself reflect one of the cultural counterfeits of justice, either harsh judgment or permissive indifference? How might Jesus be inviting you to walk the narrow road of restorative love instead?
3. How does the question, "What if this was your child?" shape the way you view those who have wronged you, or those the world deems beyond help? What does it look like for you to join the Father in His rescue?

CONCLUSION

TWO SONS, TWO NATIONS, ONE OPEN GATE

How the whole story has always been about coming home

AS WE COME TO the end of *Reconstructing Dad*, we're invited to stand at the edge of the story and look back, not just on the chapters of this book, but on the long, winding road of redemption God has been writing since the beginning.

Throughout these pages, we've traced the contours of the Father's heart through the wounds of our own stories, the faces of misunderstood characters, the reorientation of justice, and the unveiling of mercy. Now, in these final scenes, all these separate threads converge. If we have ears to hear and eyes to see, we'll find the same heartbeat pulsing through it all—the relentless, open-armed love of a Father who never stops calling His children home.

As we close, we'll walk through three sacred pictures:

- A prophet who'd rather watch an enemy nation burn than see them embraced as brothers
- A son who never left the house but somehow still missed the heart of his Father
- And an open gate at the edge of eternity, quietly insisting the way home has never been closed, at least, not from the Father's side

What these moments share is not just theological clarity, but deep personal ache. They reveal a Father who grieves estrangement even more than rebellion, and who pleads not only with sinners to come home but with saints to let go of their grudges and join the celebration.

This is the full arc of the gospel. An open gate. Just one question remains for all of us. Will we come inside?

TWO SONS

"There was a man who had two sons" (Luke 15:11).

So begins the parable we affectionately call The Prodigal Son. But from the first line, Jesus invites us to see something deeper. This is not a story about rebellion—it's a story about relationship. About family. About home.

I imagine the younger son as a teenager, tall, handsome, and charming. The kind of kid who turned heads and made parents proud, until his restlessness set in. When he asked for his inheritance, it wasn't a polite request. It was a rejection. An inheritance is something given *when someone dies*. By demanding his inheritance, this son is saying, in effect, "You're dead to me. Give me what's mine, because my bags are packed to go live my life without you."

And the father, heart shattered, let him go.

The son hit the road with pockets full and a fire in his chest. He threw himself into every pleasure he could find—parties, flings, fast friends, and faster thrills. He tried to buy happiness, companionship, maybe even a little peace. But before he knew it, the money ran out. The fun faded. And the people? They bounced the same moment his checks did. And before the door could close on their way out, he watched every last shred of self-respect leave with them. *What had he done?*

That's when it happened. He remembered.

He remembered his father. He remembered home. He thought, I've burned the bridge to ever be a son again, but maybe, just maybe, I could return as a servant. If I mind my manners and keep my head down, maybe he'll let me earn a place back.

So, he turned toward home. And this is where the story gets good.

Jesus says, "While he was still a long way off, his father saw him" (vs. 20). That can only mean one thing. His father was watching. Waiting. Hoping. Refusing to close the gate. The son had said, "You're dead to me." But the father whispered, "No son, I'd die for you."

And the second he returned, before he could rehearse his apology, before he could prove anything, the father ran. Not walked. *Ran.* He threw his arms around the one who had rejected him, bridged the distance of every wayward second, and smothered shame with mercy's embrace. Then he called for robes, rings, and sandals, the things that belonged to the prodigal, as the king's *son.* And he threw a party.

And for most of us who've heard the story, that's where the credits roll. *But it's not the end of the story,* because another son's heart had been running.

When the older brother saw the celebration, he seethed. He wouldn't even say his brother's name. "This son of yours," he spit. "All this time, I've been here, working for you, obeying you, performing for you. And you've never thrown me a party!" He tore away from the property line and turned his back from the party, refusing to move.

It is entirely possible to live under the roof of the Father yet never know His *heart.* To be the son who obeys all the rules, sing all the songs, say all the right things, but serve God like an employer, not a dad. That was the older son's posture. "I work. You reward." And now, seeing someone undeserving receive *grace*? It shattered his illusion. At this moment, the Father burned with love for this son not because of anything he had done, but because no one can earn their way to sonship. He told him, "I adore you and *everything I have is yours!*"

The father had held his son since his first breath. He'd watched his tiny feet take their first wobbly steps and walked beside them ever since. And now, in this moment, he reminded his son that he still chose him. With all his mess and all his shortcomings, he chose him. *And he chose his brother too.*

The story ends on a cliffhanger. We don't know what the older son did next. But we can be confident of where the father stood. He was right at the edge of the property line, with his arms wide open.

TWO NATIONS

Long before Jesus told a story about two sons, the word of the Lord came to a prodigal named Jonah. This time, the Father's call wasn't just for one child, but for an entire nation of them.

Nineveh, the capital of Assyria, strayed far from the life it was created to know. And so God sent Jonah to go east with a message of warning and invitation. But instead of heading 500 miles toward Nineveh, Jonah fled 2,000 miles *in the opposite direction*. Given a prophetic assignment to confront enemies, Jonah sprinted toward the farthest edge of the civilized world.[111]

It took a storm, a disastrous game of dice, a self-imposed drowning, and three days inside a fish's gut before Jonah finally reconsidered. He went to Nineveh and preached with fire. The sin they'd sown was reaping their own destruction. But then the craziest thing happened.

They *listened*.

From kings to commoners, the entire city repented in sorrow and humility. They were so serious, they even put sackcloth and ashes on their animals. You've heard of goat yoga? This was cow church! They took the word of the Lord seriously, turning from their wicked ways.

You'd think Jonah would've rejoiced. *And you'd be wrong.*

Jonah stormed out of the greatest revival in recorded history, shoving past the mourners as he fled outside the city gates. There, on the outskirts, he built a shack and sat to sulk. Maybe they'll backslide, he thought. Maybe God will change His mind. But as the city's weeping turned to relief and rejoicing, Jonah seethed. "I knew it," he lamented. "I knew you were merciful."

"He prayed to the Lord, 'Isn't this what I said, Lord, when I was still at home? That is what I tried to forestall by fleeing to Tarshish. I knew that you are a gracious and compassionate God, slow to anger and abounding in love, a God who relents from sending calamity. Now, Lord, take away my life, for it is better for me to die than to live" (Jonah 4:2–3 NIV).

Jonah's reluctance to go wasn't because he was afraid Nineveh would reject his message. He was afraid they might *repent*. And he didn't come to be part of a dysfunctional family reunion with the Assyrians. He came hoping for public execution.

But before we vilify Jonah as just another bitter prophet, we'd do well to understand the weight he carried. Nineveh wasn't just any city. It was the seat of Assyrian brutality, a regime known for burning children, mutilating captives, stacking skulls in towering monuments to fear.[112] These weren't abstract enemies. They were the monsters who had enslaved and slaughtered Jonah's people.[113]

When Jonah looked into the faces of the Ninevites, he didn't see mercy. He saw memories. Pain. Trauma. Centuries of unspeakable cruelty. In his eyes, Nineveh's repentance didn't feel like redemption. It felt like betrayal. Their tears were a mockery of the ones his own ancestors had shed. What God called compassion, Jonah called cruel.

The Hebrew text of Jonah 4:1 says it plainly. "It was evil to Jonah with great evil."[114]

Yet, just days earlier, Jonah had cried out in emotional gratitude for the mercy of God that spared his life during his own rebellious tantrum.

"The waters closed in over me to take my life; the deep surrounded me; weeds were wrapped about my head. To the roots of the mountains I went down, to the land whose bars closed upon me forever. Yet you brought up my life from the pit, O Lord my God" (Jonah 2:5–6).

It would appear that Jonah *loved* mercy, so long as it was reserved for people who looked, thought, and sinned like him. The tendency of humanity to separate into "us and them," constructing our own sacred shacks where we look for God to bless us and blast our enemies, is nothing new.

As Jonah stewed outside the city in self-righteousness, what did God do?

He came low.

God provided a leafy plant to cover Jonah from the heat of the sun, so perhaps he could relinquish the heat of his anger. But the next day, when the plant suddenly died without warning, Jonah went off the deep end. And here, God drew near one final time, not with condemnation, but with a question.

"And the Lord said, 'You pity the plant, for which you did not labor, nor did you make it grow, which came into being in a night and perished in a night. And should not I pity Nineveh, that great city, in which there are more than 120,000 persons who do not know their right hand from their left, and also much cattle?" (Jonah 4:10–11).

The book ends there. No resolution. Just a question, and a Father, standing at the edge of grace, pleading with His son to come inside.

Sound familiar?

The stories of Jonah and the elder brother in Luke 15 end the same way—with the Father extending mercy not only to the rebellious but also to the self-righteous. In both, the ones who think they've been right all along sit outside the gates of grace, arms crossed, waiting for their enemies to get what they deserve.

Jesus once said, "Those who are well have no need of a physician, but those who are sick. I came not to call the righteous, but sinners" (Mark 2:17).

That wasn't a compliment to the righteous. It was an indictment of who they *thought* they were. They had mistaken moral rigidity for holiness. Mistaking fences for faithfulness, they built barriers to keep others out and called it devotion. In their zeal to appear pure, they weaponized pride and forgot mercy.

And even still, the Father stands with arms open.

We often treat judgment as if God is gleefully separating sheep from goats, wheat from weeds. But in Jesus, we see the truth. *He is the Father who runs to both of His sons.* He is the God who weeps over wayward cities and wanders into deserts to reason with angry prophets. And when we insist on building our little booths and perching ourselves above others, He sits with us and whispers, "Please remember, you've needed mercy, too."

Ultimately, both sons need to turn. Both nations need to repent.

And at the end of all things, one gate still stands open, with the porch light on and the Father watching the horizon. He's waiting for all His children, no matter how far they've wandered, to come home.

ONE OPEN GATE

"And I saw no temple in the city, for its temple is the Lord God the

Almighty and the Lamb. And the city has no need of sun or moon to shine on it, for the glory of God gives it light, and its lamp is the Lamb. By its light will the nations walk, and the kings of the earth will bring their glory into it, and its gates will never be shut by day—and there will be no night there. They will bring into it the glory and the honor of the nations" (Revelation 21:22–26).

As the final pages of Scripture unfold, we arrive at the New Jerusalem. Unlike any kingdom since Eden, this one is marked by a breathtaking distinction. *Its gates are never shut.*

When humanity fell in the garden, flaming swords barred the way to the Tree of Life. Ever since, nations have erected walls and drawn borders, fencing off who's in and who must stay out. But now, as the Tree of Life reappears in the story for the first time since Genesis, we find no barrier in sight. The gates once closed are now open. Always.

In this final vision, Eden is not merely restored, it's *fulfilled.* Every tear sown in exile is wiped from our eyes. Every loss reversed. Every injustice redeemed. The old order is gone. All things are made new.

And over it all, one image remains. Her gates will *never* be shut.

After all the stories, all the prophecies, all the cries and wanderings and homecomings, this is the final thing the Father wants to say.

For centuries, the traditional understanding of salvation has rested on the belief that a person's response to God must occur within this lifetime. Hebrews 9:27 says man will die once and be judged after his death. Yet the very next verse reveals the true focus, "so Christ, having been offered once to bear the sins of many, will appear a second time, not to deal with sin but to save those who are eagerly waiting for him" (Hebrews 9:28).

This passage isn't a detailed sequence of postmortem events. It's a declaration of Christ's sufficiency and our dependence on Him. It is not a map of the afterlife, but a magnifying glass on Christ's finished work for any who will receive it.

This has led some to speculate on the possibility of responding in faith to Christ *after* death. Talks of purgatory, testimonies about glimpses of the other side from people declared clinically dead before returning to life, and countless theories have abounded.

I come bearing no theories or tidy answers to these questions. But I can offer three very important reflections.

First, the entire biblical narrative urges us to respond to the Father's voice today.

- "Now is the time of God's favor, now is the day of salvation" (2 Corinthians 6:2 NIV).
- "Today, if you hear his voice, do not harden your hearts" (Hebrews 3:7–8).
- "'Yet even now,' declares the Lord, 'return to me with all your heart'" (Joel 2:12–13).

We have no reason to delay. The door is open now.

Second, if our hearts do not desire to follow God here, what makes us believe we would suddenly change by extending the clock? Joshua Ryan Butler writes, "Do we get a second chance? The question often arises: 'Can I reject God now but change my mind on the threshold of his kingdom?' To ask the question this way, however, is misleading: it reveals that we probably don't actually want the kingdom. If we prefer freedom from God now, what makes us think we'll change our mind when his kingdom comes? If we harden our hearts toward his presence today, why would we expect tomorrow to be different?[115]

The human problem isn't lack of opportunity—it's *pride*. The root sin is always the same: "I will live for me." And living for me always ends in wounding someone else.

The invitation to the kingdom of God is not a doctrinal checklist or a list of moral dos and don'ts. It's the surrender of our own little kingdoms to receive a love we cannot earn. God has revealed Himself sufficiently in every corner and age of creation—being visible through all He has made, so that every heart has what it needs to turn toward Him (Romans 1:19–20). We're not called to fixate on some sadistic need to categorize who's in and who's out, but to be captivated by the God who came low in mercy for us all.

My theology is remarkably simple. Moment by moment, *every human heart* is aching for intimacy with God.

As Augustine wrote, "You have made us for yourself, O God, and our hearts are restless until they find rest in you."[116] Every one of us, younger prodigals and older ones, have chased substitutes in vain, trying to fill the ache within. And every one of us is still invited home. Which brings us here, to the end.

Third, and finally, this is what I know.

- Jesus is the way, the truth, and the life, and no one comes to the Father *except through Him*.
- God adores all that He has made.
- He is a long road of mercy.
- And His gates are never shut, because the Father's heart never closes.

I refuse to speculate beyond the beauty of His heart.

I can only agree in one thing with the pastor from my days at *Heaven's Gates, Hell's Flames*. I agree with his plea, "You don't know what is going to happen next."

But I *do* know what God is like.

I know He is good.

I know He is love.

I know He is better than we've dared to imagine.

I know His face looks exactly like Jesus.

And I know, right now, that His arms and His gates are open wide, calling all of His kids home.

This is our Father.

DISCUSSION QUESTIONS:

1. In the parables of the Prodigal Son and the story of Jonah, both "older brothers" struggle to accept the mercy extended to those they view as unworthy. Where do you see traces of the older

brother or Jonah's bitterness still hiding in your own heart?

2. The final vision in Revelation speaks of a city whose gates "will never be shut." What does this image say to you about the character of God? How does it challenge or reshape the boundaries you've been taught about who belongs in or out?
3. How has this book helped you turn toward home? What old assumptions or fears has the book invited you to unlearn? And what do you sense the Father is saying to you about His heart and your place in it?

A PRAYER TO MY FATHER

I INVITE YOU TO PRAY THIS WITH ME:

"God, I choose to receive this truth. You, my Creator, presently adore me. You made me, specifically and uniquely, in Your image, to be joined to You in intimacy, as a shadow is joined to its source. You created me to reign over creation with You. But pride and violence corrupted everything, including my own heart. The problem in the world wasn't just outside me or around me. It was within me. I have pursued pride, self-reliance, self-fulfillment, self-absorption, self-preservation, and self-help. And my pride has led me to violence. I've hurt those You've called me to love, by my actions, and by my inactions.

And I am so deeply sorry.

Yet still, You *adore* me. Before You made me, You chose me. *You came low.* Love came to town, and You tabernacled with me. You forgave me, inviting me to lay down every weapon and trust You.

You freely give Your grace, so I could be baptized into Your joy and live as a fount of Your love forever. I say, "Yes, Jesus!" A million times, I say, "Yes!"

Come and be the fullness of *my* Father.

Teach me how to love.

Lead me as I live.

Reconstruct my image of you as my Father, and me as your Beloved.

And I will dance in this truth and give it away for all eternity.

Amen.

ACKNOWLEDGMENTS

WHERE DO I EVEN BEGIN? This project has been the longest of my literary life: eight years in coming to fruition. There were many days I wondered if this book would ever find its way into your hands.

Thank you to ***my dads*** who I dedicated this book to. You have changed my life.

Thank you to my wife, ***Jill,*** who is my closest friend and my constant cheerleader. I simply cannot imagine life without you…and I don't want to!

Thank you to my amazing kids: ***Bradley, Josiah, Gabriel, Andrew,*** and ***Annabelle.*** One of the greatest joys of my life is being your dad. I am incredibly proud of the unique and amazing expressions of the "hope of glory" you each carry! Know your dad is forever proud of you!

Thank you to my literary agent and my dear friend, ***Cheryl Ricker*** (and ***Dwight***)! You have been my champion, my advocate, and a catalyst who has helped me grow tremendously as an author and as a person. I am so grateful for you!

Thank you to ***Tami, DeeDee, Andy, Deb*** and the entire ***CrossRiver Media team***! You took a chance on me by bringing me in as the first-ever male author to this beautiful literary family. It is an honor I don't take lightly. I have been blown away by your love for Jesus and one another, and by the standard of excellence you've carried in every step of this book's publication. I'm grateful to be part of the CrossRiver family!

Thank you to my sweet friend, ***Niki Hathorn***, who plugged away as a research assistant through some of the weightiest topics I undertook here. Your notes and encouragement mean more to me than I can express.

Thank you to ***my mom*** for SO many hours listening to drafts of the book in its various stages of development. It was your enthusiasm and hunger that let me know early on I was onto something that needed to be shared. I love you!

Thank you to ***Brit, Bill,*** and ***George*** for your continual encouragement, but also your compassionate ear as I tried to navigate which way to go on bringing this book to the world.

Thank you to ***the pastors and family of Overflow Church***! You guys are just my favorite. To ***my co-pastors***, there's no one I'd rather run arm-in-arm with in this beautiful adventure we get to share. To the ***members of Overflow***, thank you for receiving me as your Pastor and loving me as your brother.

Thank you, ***Little Everglades Ranch and Retreat*** (and my dear friends ***Bart and Charity Rice***) for providing the perfect place to get away for my final preparations for the book. (And thank you to the ***generous friends*** who sacrificed from their own pockets to send me: you know who you are!)

Finally, thank you to ***my King, my Savior, my Friend,*** and ***my Father.*** You are my whole world. Thank you for continually opening doors for me to tell people just how wonderful You are. This heart is yours, forever.

ABOUT THE AUTHOR

CHUCK AMMONS IS a father, husband, pastor, author, songwriter, and friend whose greatest passion is helping people encounter the goodness of God as Father and discover the greatness of their unique voice in His kingdom.

Fatherhood has shaped every part of Chuck's life and calling. After spending many years wrestling under a worldview marked by fear and shame, he experienced a profound awakening to God's love for him as Father—an encounter that didn't just change his beliefs, but transformed his identity and redirected his ministry. Chuck is the proud dad of five incredible kids, a foster dad who has had the joy of partnering with Jesus in the restoration of broken families, and a spiritual father to sons and daughters across the globe. At the heart of his message and ministry is a simple, hope-filled conviction: God is ridiculously good, and He is relentlessly in love with all He has made.

Chuck has been married to his high school sweetheart, Jill, since 2002. She is his very best friend, his partner in ministry, and the love of his life. Jill radiates the love of Jesus, anchors their family, and brings more laughter into Chuck's life than anyone else on the planet.

Since 1998, Chuck has had the joy of serving in the local church, and he has been in leadership within the same congregation since 2001. He currently serves as Pastor and Lead Visionary at Overflow Church, while also being a passionate advocate for unity among the churches of the Tampa Bay area—a place he and Jill are grateful to call home. As a pastor and teacher, Chuck carries a father's heart and a communicator's gift, helping people see God clearly, live from beloved identity, and walk in freedom, purpose, and joy.

Chuck is the author of eight books, with several more on the way. Through his writing, he seeks to bring perspective, passion, and perseverance to those longing for a deeper, more grounded faith. His work consistently points readers back to the finished work of Jesus, the transforming love of the Father, and the gentle, faithful work of the Holy Spirit—awakening hearts to beloved identity and calling forth the unique voice God has placed within every son and daughter.

He is also a member of the singer-songwriter group Valley's End, where he writes, records, and performs songs of hope alongside some of his closest friends—another expression of his love for creativity, community, and honest storytelling.

Above all else, Chuck desires to be faithful as he runs after Jesus—and to walk alongside others as a friend on the journey. His hope is that every encounter, whether through a book, a song, a message, or a conversation, feels like fresh wind in the sails. He is honored to be part of the CrossRiver family!

ENDNOTES

ONE

1. John Eldredge, *Wild at Heart: Field Manual* (Thomas Nelson, 2002), 32.

2. Stephen Baskerville, "Is There Really a Fatherhood Crisis?" *The Independent Review* (Spring 2004), accessed November 4, 2023, https://www.independent.org/publications/tir/article.asp?id=35.

3. Leif Hetland, *Healing the Orphan Spirit* (Global Mission Awareness, 2013), 3.

4. Strong's G27 – agapētos," *BibleHub*, accessed November 5, 2023, https://biblehub.com/greek/27.htm.

TWO

5. Greg A. Boyd, *Cross Vision: How the Crucifixion of Jesus Makes Sense of Old Testament Violence* (Fortress Press, 2018), 9.

6. Richard Dawkins, *The God Delusion* (Black Swan, 2008), 31.

7. "What's 96 Percent of the Universe Made Of? Astronomers Don't Know," Space.com, accessed November 6, 2023, https://www.space.com/11642-dark-matter-dark-energy-4-percent-universe-panek.html.

THREE

8. *An Unreal Dream: The Michael Morton Story*, directed by Al Reinert (CNN Films, 2013).

9. *An Unreal Dream: The Michael Morton Story*, Amazon listing, accessed December 29, 2023, https://www.amazon.com/Unreal-Dream-Michael-Morton-Story/dp/B011KKDNGG.

10. Strong's G3708 – horaō," *BibleHub*, accessed December 29, 2023, https://biblehub.com/greek/3708.htm.

11. Strong's G1097 – ginōskō," *BibleHub*, accessed December 29, 2023, https://biblehub.com/greek/1097.htm.

12. Strong's G1166 – deiknymi," *BibleHub*, accessed December 29, 2023, https://biblehub.com/greek/1166.htm.

13. Strong's G541 – apaugasma," *BibleHub*, accessed December 29, 2023, https://biblehub.com/greek/541.htm.

14. Michael Ramsey, *God, Christ, and the World: A Study in Contemporary Theology* (SCM, 1969), 9.

FOUR

15. Strong's H3068 – YHWH," *BibleHub*, accessed January 5, 2024, https://biblehub.com/hebrew/3068.htm.

16. Strong's H410 – *'ēl*," *BibleHub*, accessed January 5, 2024, https://biblehub.com/hebrew/410.htm.

17. Strong's H7355 – *rāḥam*," *Blue Letter Bible*, accessed January 5, 2024, https://www.blueletterbible.org/lexicon/h7355/kjv/wlc/0-1/.

18. Strong's H2587 – *ḥannûn*," *Blue Letter Bible*, accessed January 6, 2024, https://www.blueletterbible.org/lexicon/h2587/kjv/wlc/0-1/.

19. Strong's H2603 – *ḥānan*," *Blue Letter Bible*, accessed January 6, 2024, https://www.blueletterbible.org/lexicon/h2603/kjv/wlc/0-1/.

20. Strong's H750 – *'ārēḵ*," and "Strong's H748 – *'āraḵ*," *Blue Letter Bible*, accessed January 6, 2024, https://www.blueletterbible.org/lexicon/h750/kjv/wlc/0-1/; https://www.blueletterbible.org/lexicon/h748/kjv/wlc/0-1/.

21. Strong's H2617 – *ḥeseḏ*," *Blue Letter Bible*, accessed January 6, 2024, https://www.blueletterbible.org/lexicon/h2617/kjv/wlc/0-1/.

22. Strong's H539 – *'āman*," *Blue Letter Bible*, accessed January 6, 2024, https://www.blueletterbible.org/lexicon/h539/kjv/wlc/0-1/.

23. Strong's H5341 – *nāṣar*," *Blue Letter Bible*, accessed January 6, 2024, https://www.blueletterbible.org/lexicon/h5341/kjv/wlc/0-1/.

24. Strong's H5771 – *'āwōn*," *Blue Letter Bible*, accessed January 6, 2024, https://www.blueletterbible.org/lexicon/h5771/kjv/wlc/0-1/.

25. Strong's H6588 – *peša'*," *Blue Letter Bible*, accessed January 6, 2024, https://www.blueletterbible.org/lexicon/h6588/kjv/wlc/0-1/.

26. Strong's H2403 – *ḥaṭṭā't*," *Blue Letter Bible*, accessed January 6, 2024, https://www.blueletterbible.org/lexicon/h2403/kjv/wlc/0-1/.

27. Strong's H5375 – *nāśā'*," *Blue Letter Bible*, accessed January 6, 2024, https://www.blueletterbible.org/lexicon/h5375/kjv/wlc/0-1/.

28. "Why Do Humans Keep Inventing Gods to Worship?" *Psychology Today*, July 6, 2021, accessed January 6, 2024, https://www.psychologytoday.com/us/blog/your-brain-food/202107/why-do-humans-keep-inventing-gods-worship.

FIVE

29. Strong's H4390 – *mālā'*," *Blue Letter Bible*, accessed March 6, 2026, https://www.blueletterbible.org/lexicon/h4390/kjv/wlc/0-1/.

30. Strongs H4390, mālā'. https://www.blueletterbible.org/lexicon/h4390/kjv/wlc/0-1/. Accessed 3/6/26.

31. Strong's G1228 – diabolos," *Blue Letter Bible*, accessed January 6, 2024, https://www.blueletterbible.org/lexicon/g1228/kjv/tr/0-1/.

32. Strong's H7854 – *śāṭān*," *BibleHub*, accessed January 6, 2024, https://biblehub.com/hebrew/7854.htm.

33. Strong's H1361 – *gāḇah*," *Blue Letter Bible*, accessed January 6, 2024, https://www.blueletterbible.org/lexicon/h1361/kjv/wlc/0-1/.

34. Strong's H2555 – *ḥāmās*," *Blue Letter Bible*, accessed January 6, 2024, https://www.blueletterbible.org/lexicon/h2555/kjv/wlc/0-1/.

35. For a complete list of the sixty references to "*ḥāmās*" in the Old Testament and their meanings, see author's website. .

36. See, for example, Ps. 27:12; 35:11; 55:9; 140:1, 4; Hab. 1:2–3.

37. See, for example, 2 Sam. 22:3, 49; Ps. 18:48; 72:14.

38. Strong's G538 – apataō," *Blue Letter Bible*, accessed January 6,

2024, https://www.blueletterbible.org/lexicon/g538/kjv/tr/0-1/.

SIX

39. Strong's G135 – ainigma," *BibleHub*, accessed December 29, 2023, https://biblehub.com/greek/135.htm.

40. Cain" (Strong's H7014), from "Strong's H7013 – qayin," meaning "weapon" or "spear," *BibleHub*, accessed December 29, 2023, https://biblehub.com/hebrew/7013.htm.

41. Bruce K. Waltke, *Genesis: A Commentary* (Zondervan, 2001), 96.

42. Strong's H7451 – *ra'*," *Blue Letter Bible*, accessed December 29, 2023, https://www.blueletterbible.org/lexicon/h7451/kjv/wlc/0-1/.

43. Strong's H5162 – *nāḥam*," *Blue Letter Bible*, accessed December 29, 2023, https://www.blueletterbible.org/lexicon/h5162/kjv/wlc/0-1/.

44. Strong's H6087 – *'āṣaḇ*," *Blue Letter Bible*, accessed December 29, 2023, https://www.blueletterbible.org/lexicon/h6087/kjv/wlc/0-1/.

45. Gregory A. Boyd, *Cross Vision: How the Crucifixion of Jesus Makes Sense of Old Testament Violence* (Fortress Press, 2018), 197.

46. Strong's H3381 – *yāraḏ*," *Blue Letter Bible*, accessed December 29, 2023, https://www.blueletterbible.org/lexicon/h3381/kjv/wlc/0-1/.

47. "The Exodus Plagues: Judgment on Egypt's Gods," *Beyond Today*, March 5, 2019, accessed December 29, 2023, https://www.ucg.org/beyond-today/beyond-today-magazine/the-exodus-plagues-judgment-on-egypts-gods.

SEVEN

48. Baal, Asherah, and the God of Everything," *Leaders Go Last*, October 16, 2016, accessed January 6, 2024, https://leadersgolast.com/baal-asherah-god-of-everything/.

49. Walter C. Kaiser Jr. et al., *Hard Sayings of the Bible* (InterVarsity Press, 1996), 620.

50. William Paul Young, *The Shack* (Hodder & Stoughton, 2008), 121–22.

51. Brian Zahnd, *Sinners in the Hands of a Loving God* (WaterBrook, 2017), 25–26.

52. For discussion of how early church fathers often interpreted the gospel through a nonviolent lens—contrasting with later interpretations shaped by political and social power—see Gregory A. Boyd, *The Crucifixion of the Warrior God: Interpreting the Old Testament's Violent Portraits of God in Light of the Cross* (Fortress Press, 2017).

EIGHT

53. Strong's G264 – hamartanō," *Blue Letter Bible*, accessed January 6, 2024, https://www.blueletterbible.org/lexicon/g264/kjv/tr/0-1/.

54. Eric Clapton, quoted in "Eric Clapton Quotes," AZQuotes, accessed January 6, 2024, https://www.azquotes.com/quote/629087.

55. Strong's H1288 – *bāraḵ*," *Blue Letter Bible*, accessed October 16, 2025, https://www.blueletterbible.org/lexicon/h1288/kjv/wlc/0-1/.

56. Strong's G4434 – ptōchos," *Blue Letter Bible*, accessed January 6, 2024, https://www.blueletterbible.org/lexicon/g4434/kjv/tr/0-1/.

57. Strong's G3996 – pentheō," *Blue Letter Bible*, accessed January 6, 2024, https://www.blueletterbible.org/lexicon/g3996/kjv/tr/0-1/.

58. Strong's G4239 – praus," *Blue Letter Bible*, accessed January 6, 2024, https://www.blueletterbible.org/lexicon/g4239/kjv/tr/0-1/.

59. Strong's G1343 – dikaiosynē," *Blue Letter Bible*, accessed January 6, 2024, https://www.blueletterbible.org/lexicon/g1343/kjv/tr/0-1/.

60. Strong's G1653 – eleeō," *Blue Letter Bible*, accessed January 6, 2024, https://www.blueletterbible.org/lexicon/g1653/kjv/tr/0-1/.

61. Strong's G2513 – katharos," *Blue Letter Bible*, accessed January 6, 2024, https://www.blueletterbible.org/lexicon/g2513/kjv/tr/0-1/.

62. Strong's G1518 – eirēnopoios," *Blue Letter Bible*, accessed January 6, 2024, https://www.blueletterbible.org/lexicon/g1518/kjv/tr/0-1/.

63. Strong's G3710 – orgizō," *Blue Letter Bible*, accessed January 6, 2024, https://www.blueletterbible.org/lexicon/g3710/kjv/tr/0-1/.

64. Strong's G4469 – raka," *Blue Letter Bible*, accessed January 6, 2024, https://www.blueletterbible.org/lexicon/g4469/kjv/tr/0-1/.

65. Strong's G1937 – epithymeō," *Blue Letter Bible*, accessed January 6, 2024, https://www.blueletterbible.org/lexicon/g1937/kjv/tr/0-1/.

66. Mishnah Gittin 9:10 (compiled by Rabbi Judah HaNasi, ca. 200 CE).

67. Gregory A. Boyd, *Cross Vision: How the Crucifixion of Jesus Makes Sense of Old Testament Violence* (Fortress Press, 2018), 73.

68. Exod. 21:24; Lev. 24:20; Deut. 19:21.

69. Strong's G436 – anthistēmi," *Blue Letter Bible*, accessed January 7, 2024, https://www.blueletterbible.org/lexicon/g436/kjv/tr/0-1/.

70. Community Rule (1QS 6–7), in The Dead Sea Scrolls.

NINE

71. Strong's G2041 – ergon," *Blue Letter Bible*, accessed March 7, 2024, https://www.blueletterbible.org/lexicon/g2041/kjv/tr/0-1/.

72. Strong's G1067 – geenna," *Blue Letter Bible*, accessed March 8, 2024, https://www.blueletterbible.org/lexicon/g1067/kjv/tr/0-1/.

73. Leland Ryken, James C. Wilhoit, and Tremper Longman III, eds., *Dictionary of Biblical Imagery*, s.v. "Hell" (InterVarsity Press, 1998), 376.

74. Merrill C. Tenney, ed., *The Zondervan Pictorial Encyclopedia of the Bible, vol. 2* (Zondervan, 1975), 671; R. F. Youngblood, ed., Nelson's *New Illustrated Bible Dictionary* (Thomas Nelson Publishers, 1995), 568.

75. The primary meaning of the word translated "condemned" here is "to separate." Here, Jesus warns them of separating themselves from the grace he freely offered.

76. Strong's G86 – hadēs," *Blue Letter Bible*, accessed March 8, 2024, https://www.blueletterbible.org/lexicon/g86/kjv/tr/0-1/.

77. Strong's H7585 – *šĕʾôl*," *Blue Letter Bible*, accessed March 8, 2024, https://www.blueletterbible.org/lexicon/h7585/kjv/wlc/0-1/.

78. See, for example, NIV, ESV, NASB, HCSB, NET, AMP.

79. Strong's G5020 – tartaroō," *Blue Letter Bible*, accessed March 8, 2024, https://www.blueletterbible.org/lexicon/g5020/kjv/tr/0-1/.

80. Strong's G2849 – kolazō," *Blue Letter Bible*, accessed October 18, 2025, https://www.blueletterbible.org/lexicon/g2849/kjv/tr/0-1/.

81. C. S. Lewis, *The Problem of Pain* (HarperOne, 1996), 130.

TEN

82. "Jonathan Edwards and Sinners in the Hands of an Angry God," *Enfield Historical Society*, accessed October 20, 2025, https://enfieldhistoricalsociety.org/old-town-hall/jonathan-edwards-and-sinners-in-the-hands-of-an-angry-god/.

83. "Jonathan Edwards: Preaching in the Power of the Holy Spirit," I*nstitute in Basic Life Principles*, accessed October 20, 2025, https://iblp.org/jonathan-edwards-preaching-in-the-power-of-the-holy-spirit/.

84. Brian Zahnd, *Sinners in the Hands of a Loving God* (Colorado Springs: WaterBrook, 2017), 6.

85. Strong's G3107 – makarios," *Blue Letter Bible*, accessed May 15, 2025, https://www.blueletterbible.org/lexicon/g3107/kjv/tr/0-1/.

86. Zahnd, *Sinners in the Hands of a Loving God*, 173.

87. Strong's G1343 – dikaiosynē," *Blue Letter Bible*, accessed March 8, 2024, https://www.blueletterbible.org/lexicon/g1343/kjv/tr/0-1/.

88. Zahnd, *Sinners in the Hands of a Loving God*, 177–78.

ELEVEN

89. Thomas Aquinas, *Commentary on the Gospel of Matthew*, trans. Fabian Larcher, O.P., and James A. Weisheipl, O.P. (Magi Books, 1973).

90. Strong's H4941 – *mišpāṭ*," *Blue Letter Bible*, accessed March 4, 2024, https://www.blueletterbible.org/lexicon/h4941/kjv/wlc/0-1. (There are 424 occurrences of *mišpāṭ* in the Old Testament.)

91. Strong's H6662 – *ṣadîq*," *Blue Letter Bible*, accessed March 4, 2024, https://www.blueletterbible.org/lexicon/h6662/kjv/wlc/0-1/. (Along with related terms from Strong's H6662, there are 366 occurrences of the *ṣadîq* word family in the Old Testament.)

92. Strong's G1343 – dikaiosynē," *Blue Letter Bible*, accessed March 4, 2024, https://www.blueletterbible.org/lexicon/g1343/kjv/tr/0-1/. (Along with related terms from Strong's G1343, there are 231 occurrences of the dikaiosynē word family in the New Testament.)

93. Strong's H8199 – *šāpaṭ*," *Blue Letter Bible*, accessed March

4, 2024, https://www.blueletterbible.org/lexicon/h8199/kjv/wlc/0-1/. (Along with related terms from Strong's H8199, there are 222 occurrences of the *šāpaṭ* word family in the Old Testament.)

94. Strong's G2919 – krinō," *Blue Letter Bible*, accessed March 4, 2024, https://www.blueletterbible.org/lexicon/g2919/kjv/tr/0-1/. (Along with related terms from Strong's G2919, there are 207 occurrences of the krinō word family in the New Testament.)

95. Oliver O'Donovan, quoted in *Nicholas Wolterstorff, Justice: Rights and Wrongs* (Princeton University Press, 2008), 72.

96. See Exod. 2:23–25; 3:7–9; 12:22–23; Deut. 15:9; 24:14–15; Ps. 9:12; 10:17–18; 34:14; Isa. 5:7; Hab. 1:2.

97. Scriptural accounts of the sins of Sodom and Gomorrah beyond Genesis are sobering. See Isa. 3:9; Jer. 23:14; Ezek. 16:49–50. One-fifth of the books of the Bible reference Sodom and Gomorrah as a primary example of the kind of violence God opposes (Gen.; Deut.; Isa.; Jer.; Lam.; Ezek.; Amos; Zeph.; Matt.; Luke; Rom.; 2 Pet.; Jude; Rev.).

98. "Openness to Jesus Isn't the Problem—the Church Is," *Barna Group*, May 17, 2023, accessed March 6, 2024, https://www.barna.com/research/openness-to-jesus/.

99. Strong's H2114 – zûr," *Blue Letter Bible*, accessed March 6, 2024, https://www.blueletterbible.org/lexicon/h2114/kjv/wlc/0-1/.

TWELVE

100. Strong's G3983 – peinaō," *Blue Letter Bible*, accessed March 7, 2024, https://www.blueletterbible.org/lexicon/g3983/kjv/tr/0-1/.

101. Strong's G1372 – dipsaō," *Blue Letter Bible*, accessed March 7, 2024, https://www.blueletterbible.org/lexicon/g1372/kjv/tr/0-1/.

102. Strong's G3581 – xenos," *Blue Letter Bible*, accessed March 7, 2024, https://www.blueletterbible.org/lexicon/g3581/kjv/tr/0-1/.

103. Strong's G1131 – gymnos," *Blue Letter Bible*, accessed March 7, 2024, https://www.blueletterbible.org/lexicon/g1131/kjv/tr/0-1/.

104. Strong's G770 – astheneō," *Blue Letter Bible*, accessed March 7, 2024, https://www.blueletterbible.org/lexicon/g770/kjv/tr/0-1/.

105. Strong's G5438 – phylakē," *Blue Letter Bible*, accessed March 7, 2024, https://www.blueletterbible.org/lexicon/g5438/kjv/tr/0-1/.

106. "When Pharaoh's Heart Grew Harder," *BibleProject*, accessed March 7, 2024, https://bibleproject.com/articles/pharaohs-heart-grew-harder/.

107. C. S. Lewis, *The Weight of Glory* (HarperOne, 2001), 45–46.

108. Strong's G3874 – paraklēsis," *Blue Letter Bible*, accessed March 7, 2024, https://www.blueletterbible.org/lexicon/g3874/kjv/tr/0-1/. See also "Strong's G3875 – paraklētos," *Blue Letter Bible*, accessed March 7, 2024, https://www.blueletterbible.org/lexicon/g3875/kjv/tr/0-1/.

109. Strong's G3809 – paideia," *Blue Letter Bible*, accessed March 7, 2024, https://www.blueletterbible.org/lexicon/g3809/kjv/tr/0-1/.

110. Brian Zahnd, "When America Went to Hell," June 8, 2013, accessed March 7, 2024, https://brianzahnd.com/2013/06/when-america-went-to-hell/.

CONCLUSION

111. Billy K. Smith and Frank S. Page, *Amos, Obadiah, Jonah, New American Commentary* (Broadman & Holman, 1995), 228.

112. Smith and Page, *Amos, Obadiah, Jonah*, 227.

113. R. F. Youngblood, F. F. Bruce, and R. K. Harrison, *Nelson's New Illustrated Bible Dictionary*, s.v. "Assyria" (Thomas Nelson, 1995), 134.

114. Strong's H7489 – *rāʿaʿ*," *Blue Letter Bible*, accessed March 7, 2024, https://www.blueletterbible.org/lexicon/h7489/kjv/wlc/0-1/.

115. Joshua Ryan Butler, *The Skeletons in God's Closet: The Mercy of Hell, the Surprise of Judgment, the Hope of Holy War* (Thomas Nelson, 2014), 163.

116. Augustine, Confessions 1.1.5.

DIVINE
DETOUR
The path you'd never choose can lead
to the faith you've always wanted.
"encouraging"
"life altering"
"Excellent!"
"a must read"
"highly recommend"
Available in bookstores and from online retailers.
CrossRiver Media
www.crossrivermedia.com

Thank you so much for reading *Reconstructing Dad.*

We hope it inspired you to grow in your faith.

If you have a minute, would you consider leaving an honest review of *Reconstructing Dad* on your favorite book-buying platform? Every review helps others learn about this book... even star ratings can make a big difference.

You can also help spread the word about *Reconstructing Dad* by...

- Mentioning the book on social media or your blog.
- Recommending it to friends, family, your small group, book club or co-workers.
- Gifting a copy to encourage a friend.

We would love to hear directly from you about your thoughts on *Reconstructing Dad*! Send us a note from CrossRiverMedia.com. While you're there, sign up for our newsletter so we can let you know about upcoming releases, encouragement, interviews with all of our great authors.

www.ingramcontent.com/pod-product-compliance
Lightning Source LLC
Chambersburg PA
CBHW061536250926
52052CB00010B/2948
* 9 7 8 1 9 3 6 5 0 1 9 5 3 *